MAKE YOUR MORTGAGE MATTER

MAKE
YOUR
MORTGAGE
MATTER

*Control Home Financing
to Increase
Financial Stability and Wealth*

JAYE HOHMAN

HOH Logistics LLC

Author photo: High Level Headshots
Editor: Lisa Dawson, LD-ink LLC

Published by HOH Logistics LLC | www.hohlogistics.com | Plano, Texas

|·[]·|

Library of Congress Control Number: 2025901396

ISBN: 979-8-9924383-0-7 (eBook)
ISBN: 979-8-9924383-1-4 (Paperback)
ISBN: 979-8-9924383-2-1 (Hardback)

1. Business & Economics – Real Estate - Mortgages – United States
2. Business & Economics - Personal Finance – Budgeting-United States
3. Business & Economics - Industries - Financial Services – United States
I. Hohman, Jaye
II. Make Your Mortgage Matter

Printed in the United States of America

10 9 8 7 6 5 4 3 2 1

To Fly

TABLE OF CONTENTS

INTRODUCTION

In 1999, my soon to be in-laws provided my fiancée and I with a $35,000 downpayment to buy a $170,000, 4th floor walk-up, 1,000 square foot apartment in Hoboken, NJ. 33 months later we sold that home for $290,000. What a mistake that turned out to be, the first of a few real estate finance blunders.

What I know now is that we should have never sold that apartment in Hoboken. My sole intention of writing this book is to inform consumers of what I have learned over the last twenty-five years so they may avoid similar mistakes. If only we had known what is to be learned from this book!

At that time, I was working for Bear Stearns, the king company of Mortgage-Backed Securities [MBS]. My job was to sell and trade investments including Collateralized Mortgage Obligations [CMOs], derivatives of MBS, to the largest credit unions in the country. Like many banking institutions, when these credit unions had excess capital, more than they could lend, their go-to investments were mortgage products. The more sophisticated asset managers would buy CMOs, the most complex form of mortgage investments.

My knowledge about the investment advantages of CMOs would continue to grow over the next decade. I acquired a great deal of competence in these mortgage products, enough knowledge to where these institutional investors purchased tens of millions of dollars of tailor-made deals I would structure for them each month. Yet I knew very little about mortgages from the consumers' perspective. In fact, a joke amongst my colleagues and I as we were trading billions of dollars of mortgages monthly was that none of us had ever originated a single mortgage.

After the mortgage crisis in 2008 and the Great Recession I knew my investors would be flat-lined for some time. Not because of anything I sold them. But their liquidity would be non-existent and any deployment of capital into MBS would be dead for years. With the passing of the Dodd-Frank Act, which essentially nationalized the mortgage industry, the private mortgage securitization market would be absolutely crushed. And that was the subject matter of my expertise.

The next five years was very difficult. Without monthly new issuances of mortgage pools there were very few opportunities for me to make enough money to survive. What was once a thriving career on a multi-millionaire trajectory was now in peril. Much younger than most of my contemporaries, I hadn't banked nearly enough money to retire or at least semi-retire, as they already had. Unlike a large majority of the upper echelon on Wall Street, I had no Ivy League MBA to spawn a new career path in the capital markets.

Having grown up in the Midwest, I knew there were some things that were actually better outside of New York City. Not the food, though. But most other things. There are better places to raise kids, of that I was certain. It would take those same five years along with completely exhausting our hard-earned savings to convince my wife. With no state income taxes, a low unemployment rate, higher affordability, better quality of life, above average schools, and more politically aligned with my tune, Texas had more appeal than any other.

Upon moving to Texas, we rented a five bedroom house at a discount for a three year lease but continued to rent that home for over seven years. Our wonderful landlord never raised the rent even once. He acknowledged the reason. The rent was always paid on time and the house and yard were meticulously maintained as if we owned the house ourselves. Having previously been homeowners, we felt it our obligation. I dare say, we left it in better condition than when we moved into it. I attribute that to at least a partial reason why the landlord moved back into the house!

Over those seven years, the taxes and homeowners insurance would have increased. And we were not on the hook for any repairs. A hot water heater was replaced at some cost. There were a few other times when a plumber was called, and some maintenance on an air conditioning unit, all at the landlord's expense. When a problem arose, I picked up the phone and let him deal with it. Being a landlord has its issues. And being a tenant can be far less worrisome.

We purchased our next house and within a month a waste pipe under the house backed up, flooding the master bathroom and bedroom. We no longer had a landlord to call to fix everything for us. That responsibility was now ours along with the cost of repairs. The insurance deductible was nearly equivalent to two months of the rent we had been previously paying.

This is a cautionary tale about the implications of exhausting all of your savings for the cost to acquire a home, including the down payment. But it is really meant to illustrate that homeownership has its disadvantages, too. However, typically it is more advantageous to own rather than rent.

I immediately landed a job in Texas as a mortgage loan originator. It turned out that earlier mentioned joke was on me. I had traded billions of dollars of MBS and now I would be offering a few hundred thousand dollars of mortgage money directly to consumers. And since, no one has told me anything I didn't already know about mortgages from a technical perspective. But over the last decade I have had the opportunity to talk to thousands of consumers about their finances. I have also worked directly with hundreds of loan originators and managed dozens more. Throughout this time, I have learned an incredible amount of practical knowledge that is quite alarming and somewhat disturbing.

Two things stand out above all, both of which have compelled me to write this book. The first is that most consumers do not approach buying and financing a home from an investors point of view despite their agreement and the conventional wisdom that it is most likely the largest investment they will ever make. They ought to do so. And the difference is paramount to obtaining and maintaining wealth. By no means is this a book meant to urge anyone to quit their day job and become a real estate investor. It is about approaching home buying with financial literacy and the proper mindset to make the best rational decisions about their mortgages. Had I that perspective, my family would still own the home in Hoboken.

Secondly, there seems to be an industry acceptance to sustain that current misguided behavior rather than an effort to provide financial literacy on this subject. Most lending companies and their mortgage loan originators cede to the emotional decisions of borrowers. Whether passively, ignorantly, or maliciously, certainly not all but many lenders avoid a subjective review of the consumers' investment objectives of this major asset. They often avoid suggestions of this nature for fear of sounding or appearing confrontational and losing the business. And most I dare say are not qualified to do so anyway, with no formal training or licensing requirements on the matter. Despite this, most consumers assume that loan originators are suggesting mortgages that are suitable for their situation. This is not true. Lenders' advice is not commensurate with fiduciary responsibility. They must only produce a loan that fits within lending guidelines. To understand this, one must recognize there is a clear distinction between qualifying for a particular mortgage and benefiting from that mortgage.

It must be stated that although a rigorous attempt has been made to provide a thorough educational resource for residential real estate finance, there are boundless rules and regulations that are far too complex and voluminous to cover in a practical guide to mortgage finance.

Indeed, ask a dozen loan originators or underwriters the exact same question and you can be assured of getting a dozen different answers. Fannie Mae publishes their *Selling Guide*, an instruction manual of 1,173 pages for their lending guidelines. (Selling Guide, 2024) For the most accurate answers, one must often go to the source.

Along with regular changes and updates to these rules, Fannie Mae often issue white papers on interpretations of their guidelines and offer a hotline for industry professionals to speak directly with their advisors for questions regarding obscure situations when using their systems. Fannie Mae is just one of many mortgage aggregators trying to keep the loans they buy consistent and acceptable for the investors of their MBS monthly issuances. This is basic proof that mortgages are a complex topic where nothing is definitive due to the uniqueness of each loan scenario.

Mortgages are incredibly complex financial instruments. But when used properly, they encourage more financial stability and offer you the greatest opportunity to grow your wealth. You now have an opportunity to take advantage of many of their benefits with strategies that consider your future first. Life changes are a certainty so plan for it...and in the end you will be able to confidently know how to properly use mortgages to grow wealth.

Let me show you the way.

PART 1: HOUSING AFFORDABILITY

*"Most men appear never to have considered
what a house is, and are actually though
needlessly poor all their lives because they think
that they must have such a one as their
neighbors have."*

-Henry David Thoreau
WALDEN

1. The Cost of Shelter

It's a trap! The American Dream is not "to own a home."

Life, liberty and the pursuit of happiness is the dream America offers to its citizens. Owning a home may indeed offer a pathway to a better life, economic liberty and financial happiness. This is true primarily because mortgages routinely offer a natural person the most leverage of their money. How to make the best use of that concept will be made in the third and final part of this book.

First, it must be understood that owning a house can be a trap. Anyone who has owned a house would likely agree with Thoreau who observed in 1854 that it is usually a tremendous financial burden. It can be a nightmare as much as a dream. Acknowledging and preparing for the expenses of homeownership is the immediate goal.

Secondly, it must be explained how to successfully navigate the mousetrap to get to the cheese. The primary intention of this mortgage book is to explain how to properly finance a house in ways best suited for financial success. Part 2 is a complicated section but of utmost importance, suggested to be read twice even by industry professionals. The details and subtle nuances between the endless mortgage configurations are what will determine if you are swallowing processed cheese or savoring a delicate brie.

A trap is usually set by distraction and disguise. Housing affordability has most recently been incorrectly referred to as it might relate to a person's ability to save for or have a down payment. The down payment is a function of how much leverage can be applied to purchase a home. With a standard 20% down payment, the leverage is 5:1, where $1 buys you $5 of house. With only a 5% down payment, the leverage is 20:1. The result is most often likely the opposite of making the house more affordable as it results in a larger mortgage and monthly payment.

This notion that the down payment is the key to housing affordability is incorrect as it pertains to a one-time event to purchase a house while ignoring the cost of keeping that house.

For instance, if a person were to be provided a house for free, the owner still must be able to afford the ongoing costs of ownership. It is similar to suggest that to rent an apartment a deposit, such as the standard first and last months' rent, is no longer required. But the renter still must be able to afford the rental payments each and every month.

Even when a house is owned free and clear of any mortgages or other liens, annual property tax payments are required to avoid the house being foreclosed upon by the municipality. And although homeowners insurance on a property that is owned outright is not required, it would be foolish to not pay that annual expense and risk the house burning down.

More traditionally and accurately, housing affordability is measured as a percentage of income that is applied toward the cost of shelter. In its simplest form, it is a rent payment.

One component of the U.S. Bureau of Labor Statistics Consumer Price Index is Shelter, as measured by two sub-components, the rent of a primary residence and owner's equivalent rent of residences. (Consumer Expenditures and Income: Overview, 2022) Since 1965, the cost of Shelter has risen by 1,500%. Since 1987, home prices have risen fivefold, as measured by the S&P CoreLogic Case-Shiller National Home Price Index. Yet the rate of home ownership in the United States has been in a range between 63% and 69% since 1965. Just fewer than 63% of households owned a house as recently as 2016. The percentage in 2024 was again about the same as 1980. (See Exhibit 1-1)

Exhibit 1-1

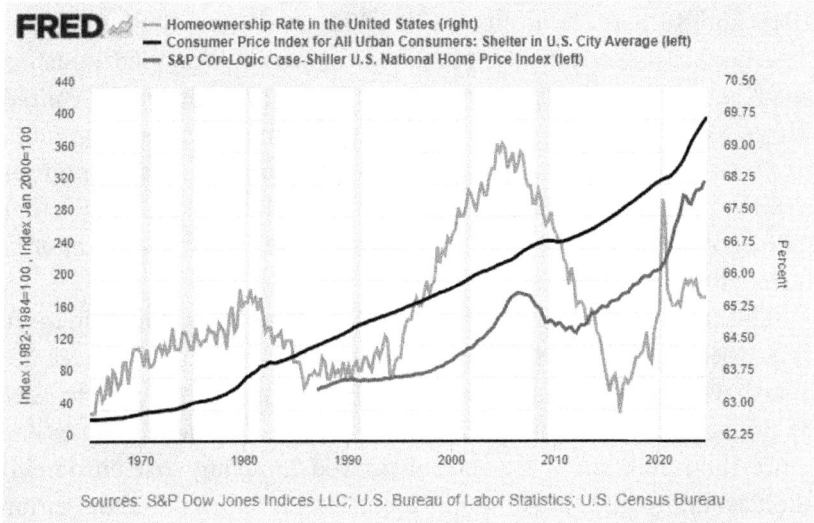

Sources: S&P Dow Jones Indices LLC; U.S. Bureau of Labor Statistics; U.S. Census Bureau

(U.S. Bureau of Labor Statistics, 2024) (S&P Dow Jones Indices LLC, 2024) (U.S. Census Bureau, 2024)

No different than providing student loans and grants to anyone that raises their hand has driven up the cost of a higher education, increasing the borrowing capability for a house has done more to increase home prices than to increase home ownership. Inflation has a lot to do with these increases, too. But, unfortunately, increasing the availability of mortgages has produced the unintended consequence of making home ownership arguably less affordable.

Research published by the Department of Housing and Urban Development clearly conveys the idea that increasing the percentage of income acceptable to be used toward shelter has a negative effect on consumers as would be expected. (U.S. Department of Housing and Urban Development Office of Policy Development and Research, 2017) Housing programs in the United States have long measured housing affordability in terms of percentage of income. In the 1940s, the maximum affordable rent for federally subsidized housing was set at 20 percent of income, which rose to 25 percent of income in 1969 and 30 percent of income in 1981. Over time, the 30 percent threshold also became the standard for owner-occupied housing, and it remains the indicator of affordability for housing in the United States. Keeping housing costs below 30 percent of income is intended to ensure that households have enough money to pay for other nondiscretionary costs; therefore, policymakers consider households who spend more than 30 percent of income on shelter to be housing cost burdened.

This same 2017 article by the HUD confirms that spending more than 30% of income on housing is detrimental to family finances. Yet less than a decade later, the same HUD continues to allow up to 50% of pre-tax income to be spent on a mortgage payment. If spending more than 30% on shelter is considered "housing cost burdened" then certainly 50% must be more burdened. Thoreau's observation in 1854 of homeowners being "needlessly poor" is likely to apply today to borrowers that borrow the most allowed rather than the most they can afford.

Additionally, this maximum 50% of income only considers the mortgage principal and interest, property taxes, homeowners insurance and association dues. This disregards many other costs that first-time home buyers have likely not considered.

The mortgage payment will be discussed thoroughly in Part 2. But first it is important to establish the other costs associated with owning a house. Without consideration, buyers might immediately be encumbered with expenses that exceed their means. In other words, they may not be able to afford those costs of which many will be unavoidable, required, and perhaps unforeseen.

2. Property Taxes

One of the traps of homeownership is the misconception that "the payment" will never go up. This is partially incorrect. It is completely true that with a traditional 30-year level pay, fixed rate mortgage, the scheduled principal & interest payment [P&I] will be the same for 360 months. And this is certainly one of the best benefits of residential real estate finance. There is little if anything else that can be negotiated so far in advance. Imagine what a hotel room might cost 30 years from now.

It is reasonably safe to say that every single other cost associated with owning a house will increase each year. But that is not meant to discourage homeownership. Because it is also just as likely that leasing a house or apartment will also be subject to annual rental payment increases as a consequence of the landlord's inflation-driven rising expenses.

Property tax increases might be controllable to some extent when voting in local elections. For instance, in Texas where public school budgets may be partially funded through bond issuances. Those are voted on by residents whether a homeowner or not. Likewise, local government administrations control their own budget spending and those dollars are derived in part from property taxes. Their fiscal policy decisions with regard to schools, capital improvements, and economic development can have significant impacts on real estate value.

Accordingly, property tax rates can vary even within city limits depending on the organization of school districts and county lines, to name a few reasons. Property taxes are

<u>Exhibit 2-1</u>

How High Are Property Taxes in Your State?

Property Taxes Paid as a Percentage of Owner-Occupied Housing Value, 2022

0.26%   2.08%

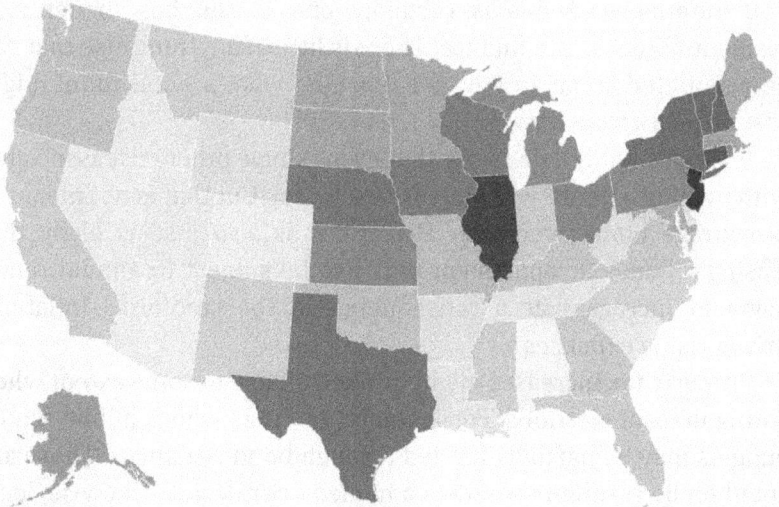

Note: The figures in this table are mean effective property tax rates on owner-occupied housing (total real taxes paid/total home value). As a result, the data exclude property taxes paid by businesses, renters, and others. DC's rank does not affect states' ranks, but the figure in parentheses indicates where it would rank if included.
Source: US Census Bureau, *2022 American Community Survey*; Tax Foundation calculations.

TAX FOUNDATION

(Yushkov, 2024)

typically assessed by each county within each state annually or less often. And, naturally, property tax rates vary widely from state to state (see Exhibit 1-2). The due date varies sometimes from county to county and often from state to state, too. Property taxes may be due quarterly, semi-annually, or annually.

That there is a tax rate is a function of taxes being assessed according to the value, "ad valorem," of each property. The rate itself is a millage rate, where "millesimum" is a thousandth in Latin, and so one mill is $1 per thousand dollars of value.

The mill rate is multiplied by the assessed value to determine the annual property taxes. The assessed value has two components, the land value and the improvements. Obviously, the improvements are any structures built on the property. Periodically, if not annually, the county tax assessor may reassess the value of each property. But note, this assessed value is not a market value nor should it be considered an appraised value, but a separate value independent from what the home may actually sell for in the open market. Generally speaking, the assessed value is based on the type of construction, square footage and room plans of the house without any consideration to the interior elements and condition of the house nor even the landscaping.

The regulations may vary from state to state but often any increase in assessed value may be capped at a certain percentage on an annual basis. These restrictions limit the increase in property taxes for each home on a yearly basis. Most states offer a limited discount on the property taxes for a primary residence as opposed to a second home or investment property. Many states also limit or restrict increases in property taxes based on the age of the homeowner or offer other exemption programs for certain types of borrowers like disabled veterans.

However, when a home is sold, the assessment value will be equivalent to the sales price. Therefore, it is important to recognize that the annual taxes paid on a home for sale may be vastly different than the amount payable by the new home owner. This is especially true on any new construction house in a new development. But there may also may be a big difference from one owner to the next on an existing home, too. This will depend on the previous sales price, any annual percentage limitations, discounts or exemptions, and to a great degree on how long the previous owner had held the property.

Indeed, it is crucial to recognize this and properly estimate what the taxes will be when budgeting for an escrow account or independently saving money to be paid when the property taxes come due. This is not to be taken lightly and can put new homeowners in a precarious situation when done incorrectly.

Property taxes and the hazard or homeowners insurance is usually paid along with the mortgage principal and interest payment. These additional funds are put into an escrow or impound account. This is essentially a savings account designed to have the amount due available when due to the county or insurance company. When an escrow account is arranged by the mortgage lender, the loan servicing company will pay those amounts on behalf of the borrower.

This can be a worthwhile and prudent service for the borrower who then must only be concerned with one total payment obligation each month rather than multiple payments due monthly and/or at different intervals throughout the year. As such, it is advisable for borrowers on a regular, salaried or fixed income but may be less helpful for commission based or seasonal wage earners who might have months with thin earnings.

For certain types of loans, like FHA, VA, and any mortgage loan exceeding 80% of the home value, an escrow or impound account is generally required.

Although a tax certification is obtained by a title company to calculate the monthly amount to be impounded for property taxes and homeowners insurance, it is not always reliable for reasons mentioned earlier. When taxes on a new home purchase are higher than expected, when they are raised, and when homeowners insurance premiums rise, more money monthly is required to fund the account. That new amount is determined by an audit of the escrow account that is performed by the loan servicing company. Any shortage in the account is usually made up over a twelve-month period by an increase in funds required. But consider that to stay above water, so to speak, the normal impound amount must also be increased.

One instance where this has happened in Texas is in new developments that are part of a Municipal Utility District [MUD]. Those houses are subject to a MUD tax. This is an additional piece of a property tax bill that repays a bond issued to create the water and sewer infrastructure for new developments. The tax is apportioned only to the homes that infrastructure spending supports rather than the real estate of the entire city. Therefore, the property tax can be dramatically higher than the residential real estate property tax that a city may publish.

Consider if money saved monthly for taxes were $400, but the correct amount should have been $600 and the error wasn't realized for 15 months, then the deficit would be $3,000. In an escrow account, this would be recouped over 12 months resulting in an additional $250 required each month. Therefore, the adjusted correct amount of $600 plus the $250 in arrears would result in an increase of the monthly required payment from $400 to $850, just for the property taxes alone. Incidents like this may be rare but they are not insignificant.

The property county will send an annual or more frequent notice to the homeowner and the mortgage servicer of amounts due and increases in taxes. It is imperative to review these notices or bills to make certain any budget is adjusted so that adequate cash is available for timely payment.

What is also not insignificant is the amount that property taxes increase over 30 years. Although a county's assessed value is not always akin to the market value, the increase in the assessed valued will commonly be in line with home price appreciation. It is realistic to think that governmental expenses will rise in some parity with the inflation of all other goods and services. Whether the local government will raise the mill rate or the assessed value or both, increases in property taxes are likely to be expected.

One final explanation with regard to property taxes is the amount due upon transfer of the real estate. As would be expected, the previous owner is responsible for the annual portion of the taxes due up to the day of sale. The new owner is responsible for the taxes from the settlement date forward. The title company is responsible for these calculations and managing the appropriations and/or disbursements of these funds.

3. Homeowners Insurance

Hazard insurance is most often referred to as homeowners insurance. This type of insurance will generally provide reimbursement for damage to the property caused by misfortune such as a fire. The cause of such damage is vital to what is covered and will be specifically listed on each policy. For instance, weather related flood insurance would need to be insured with a separate policy or rider. Therefore, it is very important to be thorough when discussing and purchasing a hazard policy with an experienced insurance agent. And it is advisable to have these discussions with a few agents to compare options and prices.

There are two costs associated with most types of insurance policies, including health, auto and certainly homeowners insurance. The premium is the main cost and that is paid in advance and on an ongoing basis. The price of the homeowners insurance premium will be subtly influenced by the borrower's credit and insurance claim history, also determined by the property value, amount of coverage, items covered, liability amounts, many other policy specific items, and, largely with respect to the amount of the deductible. Exhibit 3-1 shows the average cost of hazard insurance based on home value. For instance, $500,000 house at 1.84% in Florida could be expected to have an annual premium of $9,200.

The deductible is the second cost. It is the amount deducted from the reimbursement amount for any particular claim and is commonly a percentage of the coverage amount, often ranging from 1 to 5%. For instance, on a home valued at $1,000,000 with an equal coverage amount, a 1% deductible would mean that on any claim, the borrower would need to come up with the initial $10,000 (1,000,000 x .01) to pay for the repairs. The insurance company would cover the balance up to $990,000.

Exhibit 3-1

Homeowners Insurance Premium Cost (% of Market Value)			
Alabama	0.94%	Montana	0.84%
Alaska	0.33%	Nebraska	1.85%
Arizona	0.74%	Nevada	0.32%
Arkansas	0.99%	New Hampshire	0.33%
California	0.49%	New Jersey	0.39%
Colorado	1.07%	New Mexico	0.69%
Connecticut	0.54%	New York	0.58%
Delaware	0.32%	North Carolina	0.82%
Florida	1.84%	North Dakota	0.96%
Georgia	0.67%	Ohio	0.44%
Hawaii	0.40%	Oklahoma	1.68%
Idaho	0.43%	Oregon	0.34%
Illinois	0.80%	Pennsylvania	0.41%
Indiana	0.57%	Rhode Island	0.70%
Iowa	0.76%	South Carolina	0.81%
Kansas	1.41%	South Dakota	0.95%
Kentucky	1.09%	Tennessee	0.77%
Louisiana	1.43%	Texas	1.29%
Maine	0.41%	Utah	0.40%
Maryland	0.52%	Vermont	0.27%
Massachusetts	0.56%	Virginia	0.51%
Michigan	0.68%	Washington	0.48%
Minnesota	0.86%	West Virginia	0.33%
Mississippi	1.10%	Wisconsin	0.40%
Missouri	0.71%	Wyoming	0.45%

(Average Home Owners Insurance Cost, 2024)

Hazard insurance is always required at all times when there is a mortgage on a property. When financing the purchase of a home, the coverage begins on the transaction settlement date with an annual policy paid in advance. This means in addition to any down payment, a borrower will need to have the cash to pay for the first annual premium prior to or at closing.

Along with property taxes, homeowners insurance is the second component of an escrow payment and it, too, is almost certain to increase throughout the years. When subject to an escrow account, the annual premium is divided by twelve to produce the required payment amount. This is the same formula used to calculate the monthly property tax required. As an ongoing matter, it's that simple. The escrow account is a monthly savings account to fund the annual premium upon renewal.

Additional months of taxes and insurance are required by government regulators to fund the initial escrow account. These exact amounts vary based on the due dates for the property taxes and renewal date of the insurance policy. The formula dictates a monthly balance projection not to exceed or fall below certain thresholds.

Depending on the loan type and lender, an escrow account for homeowners insurance along with property taxes may be required in escrow. Typically, when it is optional, both or neither may be escrowed; however, it is uncommon to allow the borrower to elect to escrow one but not the other.

The hazard policy itself will be required to have a "mortgagee clause" whether there is an escrow account or not. This lists the lender and anyone who may later become the loan servicer by way of a line that will read "its successor and/or assigns" or simply "ISAOA" along with the loan number. This serves to protect lenders from the borrower receiving funds from a claim but not completing the necessary repairs.

When an insurance company provides a claim check, the servicer is usually also listed as a payee and will need to endorse the check along with the policy owner. The servicer has a right to confirm that the repairs have been completed prior to endorsement. The check will then be returned to the policy owner who may deposit the funds and pay any contractors for their services.

The mortgagee clause also ensures that the insurance company provide notification to the loan servicer if that policy lapses for non-payment or any other reason. Should a borrower elect to pay for the insurance policy directly but fail to do so, the servicer has the right, per the mortgage agreement, to obtain an adequate hazard policy.

The payment for the policy will then be required as an escrow payment. This is referred to as force-placed insurance. Note that the servicer is under no obligation to shop for a reasonably priced policy.

Many lenders previously charged a slightly higher interest rate to borrowers who chose not to escrow as there is an added element of risk involved to the lender should property taxes and homeowners insurance go unpaid for any period of time. However, many states disallowed this practice of charging extra. But as the risk did not go away, the cost of that risk may have become priced into all interest rates.

As described in the previous section and under the same circumstances an audit of the escrow account is not always completed by the mortgage servicer on an annual basis. When an audit is done, the catch up for the previous deficiency along with the increase in required monthly impound can amount to a substantial and sometimes overwhelming increase in the total mortgage payment.

Just like the importance of reviewing the county's annual property tax notice, it is wise to know if the insurance company has raised the annual premium on the house. Know that a homeowner may shop for and obtain a new policy at any time throughout the year. Even when premiums are paid in advance for the entire year, an insurance company is required to provide a refund for the remainder of the period when a policy is cancelled. A new policy can easily be substituted for the old policy at any time by contacting the loan servicing company. While some choose to ignore the rising cost of homeowners insurance, it is wise and often fruitful to compare rates on a regular basis.

Flood insurance may also be required on any house that is financed when the improvement or residential structure is deemed to be within the bounds of a designated flood zone. The Federal Emergency Management Agency [FEMA], an agency of the Department of Homeland Security, provides the resource to determine if a property is in a Special Flood Hazard Area [SFHA], Coastal Barrier Resources System [CBRS] or Otherwise Protected Area [OPA]. Those maps are readily available on-line and searchable by property address.

FEMA also manages the National Flood Insurance Program [NFIP] which subsidizes the risk of flood claims that are issued through traditional insurance companies. In determining the necessity of flood insurance, government mortgage programs rely on FEMA to measure if a property is in a flood zone, control the cost of the insurance, require it be obtained it from a private insurer, and then provide assistance to those insurance companies for any losses they incur in reimbursing homeowners for flood damage.

When flood insurance is required, it will be included in the escrow payment and accounted for in the same manner as property taxes and hazard insurance. And its cost, like others, can be expected to increase over time if not annually.

There are exceptions. For instance, in some coastal areas where hurricanes or tropical storms are more common insurers may limit or exclude wind damage which is otherwise included in most general homeowner's insurance policies. It is therefore worth repeating that it is imperative to fully understand the coverage and limitations of any policy proposals.

It is extremely prudent to include in a budget and save for the cost of a deductible, most especially with a limited or fixed income. A higher deductible will produce a lower annual premium. And that can be okay provided the cash for the higher deductible is available when needed.

But that time when it may be needed is unknown. It could very well be the same day or the following week after a home is purchased. And that is not unrealistic to imagine. In fact, whenever a state of emergency is declared due to a disaster, financing for home purchase and refinance transactions are halted in that defined area. Each subject property is required to be deemed undamaged or unaffected by the disaster before the transaction may be completed. If it can happen the day before, and it does, it can certainly happen the day after.

4. Property Owners' Associations

Property owners' association dues are paid directly by the homeowner. They are not included in an escrow or impound payment as part of the total mortgage payment.

Homeowners associations [HOAs], condominium associations and co-operative associations function to provide and maintain shared amenities within some developments. They also often seek to encourage a standard of quality for each property within that community.

Although HOAs are often shunned by many because of the monthly dues and sometimes special assessments, they do tend to increase the value of each of home within the community by an estimated average of $25,000 to $35,000. (Ball, 2024) The cost and value benefit can vary widely as do the amenities which can range from simple to obscene. From a simple park and some walking trails, to a clubhouse, pools, golf, tennis, stocked fishing ponds, gated entrance, marinas, private airstrips and hangars, amenities may be found to please any lifestyle.

Condominium associations can be similar with amenities similar to apartments or over-the-top luxury accommodations. Co-operatives are usually structured with a board or committee requiring an approval process in order to purchase a unit within the association, much like a membership committee.

This goal of a co-operative to maintain a standard of quality of owners may set a higher standard but ultimately wields the same result that HOAs and condo associations obtain by enforcing fines to owners who do not maintain their properties as required. Each of these types of associations will have a rulebook by which homeowners must abide. Covenants, Conditions, and Restrictions [CC&Rs] are the policies that are established, maintained and enforced by each development's association board members.

These rules may be limited by state laws forbidding potentially unconstitutional restrictions on property owners such as displaying religious items or possession of firearms. Beyond that, the CC&Rs can range as widely as the amenities. And they may be enforceable by fines, billing the homeowner for the remedy, or by civil lawsuit. Again, any enforcement action would need to be set forth in the CC&Rs but would also be governed by state laws.

Nonetheless, the nature of these covenants, conditions, and restrictions can still be as extreme as having the lawn professionally trimmed at 1-1/4" inches at all times or not allowing cats in a co-operative. As this may all be extremely different from one property association to the next, as well as one state to the next, it is only safe to suggest one ought to read the CC&Rs before purchasing a property. Likewise, one most certainly should understand any type of approval process to merely paint the exterior or put in a backyard pool before paying large sums to do so without approval from the architectural review committee of the association, should one exist.

The aggressiveness of the board to enforce the policies is also well worth considering. This can come and go along with the board members who are typically elected annually by the property owners. Each property owners' association board would manage three general functions much like the division of a government or business. They would be responsible for the rules, budget and operations. However, much of this is usually delegated to a property management company.

Perhaps more important than the CC&Rs, certainly from a financial risk perspective, is the reserve study of a property association. The reserve study is the formulation of budget to assess the estimated future costs that are the responsibility of the community association. These costs will then influence raising the regular assessment which is usually collected in the form of monthly or quarterly dues. But the reserve study, which is intended to be updated every five years, may find that a special assessment is required from time to time.

The regular budget would include the costs of ongoing operations such as daily pool maintenance and landscaping of the common grounds. It would also include monies to be allocated toward a reserve fund intended to pay foreseeable future costs such as road maintenance or a new roof on a community clubhouse. A reserve study dictates the funds necessary to cover these anticipated costs over the next twenty-five years. (Ball, 2024)

A largely inaccurate reserve study would likely result in an inadequate reserve fund. This could end up necessitating unaffordable special assessments.

Such has been the case in many condo associations throughout Florida since a state legislative change in 2022 following the partial collapse of the coastal 136-unit, 12 story Champlain Towers South on June 24, 2021, when 98 people died. Severe structural issues were identified by an engineering firm as early as 2018 and without repair were reportedly much worse in late 2020. A $15,000,000 remedial project had been planned but not yet begun prior to the collapse. As a result, the state mandated that condominium associations must maintain reserve funds able to satisfy any potential structural maintenance costs for buildings in excess of three stories.

To beef up their reserve funds, the required special assessments create problems for both homeowners and the associations themselves who do not have the funds.

Once again, this will differ from state to state. But in Texas, as an example, property associations carry a huge stick. As incredible as it may seem, property associations have the ability to foreclose on a property for non-payment of dues, annual approved special assessments and/or fines as a result of violations. Indeed, mortgage documents will require a buyer to sign that they will comply with CC&Rs of a property association for this very reason.

Of course, foreclosures ought to be recognized as an avoidable occurrence. Texas state laws require an association first provide reasonable attempts to cure the situation. They must give notice and demand restitution for any violations, they may offer a payment plan, send the item to a collection agency, report the unpaid debt to credit agencies, then provide several notices of an intention to place a lien on the property before actually doing so before finally instigating foreclosure proceedings. This civil lawsuit may result in a court imposed daily fine or a judicial foreclosure where the property is seized and sold. There are also avenues for the association to commence a nonjudicial foreclosure where the lien is sold at auction without the involvement of a court. This is more akin to a tax lien sale allowing the property owner an avenue to pay off the debt to the new lien holder who successfully purchased it at auction. (Property Owners' Associations, 2024)

Any and all of these enforcement policies by the property association must be defined and stated within the association's governing documents and filed with the county in order to be acted upon. Reading the articles of incorporation, bylaws, covenants, conditions, and restrictions and also an awareness of the state laws is important to truly understand the risk involved in real estate property rights, limitations and ownership risk within a property association.

The mortgage servicing company may also be notified when any of the previously stated actions are taken by an association in an attempt to collect non-payment of assessments. As the associations actions could result in a lien and foreclosure, the mortgage servicer has an immediate interest in these matters. It could be expected that they become involved in efforts to cure the issue but may have limited means to do so.

Financing residential real estate within a property association is generally subject to a review by the lender of the governing documents and financials as this information ought to be known by any potential buyer, too. Both parties ought to be concerned with the same potential issues.

Property associations that don't meet certain standards may be ineligible for traditional financing if deemed "unwarrantable." These standards are more commonly associated with condominium and co-operatives but may often and ought to be vetted for single family residences in homeowners associations, too. The exact merits may change but are generally concerned with the financial soundness of the property association, tying back to the potential of a special assessment that some if not many owners within the community may not be able to afford.

10% is an easy standard to remember. The reserve fund must be adequately funded generally with 10% or more of the regular assessment allocated to those savings as per the annual budget. And for this to be effective, owners must actually be paying those dues. If more than 10% of owners are behind in their dues or 10% of the budget is unfunded because dues are in arrears, then the financial condition of the association may be suspect.

The concentration of investor-owned properties is another area of concern fraught with many potential negative ramifications. As few as 10% of the units within an association may be owned by a single investor, but that may be up to 20% in larger developments of more than 20 units. Additionally, the percentage of units that are not owner-occupied can be concerning as those dues may be less likely to be paid in times of economic stress.

For new developments, the percentage of units completed and sold can present certain financial risks to property associations. Generally, the common areas and amenities would be developed first. And the ongoing cost to maintain those amenities must be met.

In the late 2000s this became a widespread problem caused by a confluence of events including the rapid downturn in the housing market. The issue was especially prevalent in Florida where housing construction had been booming. For a lower price and availability, home builders more frequently used imported drywall that was susceptible to mold and rot in the Floridian humidity. These issues developed quickly and builders had to replace the sheetrock with higher quality materials at a substantial expense. At the same time, the economy collapsed and recently completed homes went unsold. The combination of circumstances created a liquidity crisis for many developers who eventually declared bankruptcy. As a result, the owners of homes within the uncompleted developments had to pay for a disproportionate amount of their HOA budget that was meant to be shared by a higher number of completed units. This supports an argument that it may be very prudent to assess the financial wherewithal of a developer when purchasing in a new development.

Another financial concern would be any pending litigation that may result in an extreme financial judgement against the association requiring a special assessment to all property owners, the sum of which might be unknown but, again, potentially unaffordable.

The insurance kept by the association is next on the list. Akin to a homeowners insurance policy, each property association would be expected to hold a hazard insurance policy for community property and common areas. Condominium and co-operatives have a more extensive insurance structure. For these properties, homeowners hazard policies insure property within the shared walls, while the association policy coverage is responsible for the shared walls, ceilings, roofs, common spaces, and other exterior components. Therefore, condo and co-op dues are generally more expensive as the insurance is higher while the owners' hazard insurance policies are proportionately less.

Associations must also have adequate flood insurance for any common structures within a flood zone. And a fidelity bond insures against loss and damage as a result of inappropriate employee actions such as theft or fraud.

Despite what may be too limiting for many, HOAs are becoming increasingly less avoidable. It has become apparent that city managers throughout the United States have realized the benefits that Planned Unit Developments [PUDs] offer to them. PUDs are the domain of HOAs who relieve cities of many responsibilities and costs that may otherwise be under their jurisdiction.

Simply maintaining a respectable appearance of the homes within a PUD is a benefit to the city. The HOA will field complaints and deal with a certain house's untidiness, for instance. Those are resources a city does not have to allocate. Additionally, if a new housing development has a community pool and park, there will be less demand for such public amenities.

Gated communities offer an even greater savings for the city. The maintenance of roads and sidewalks within these developments are the responsibility of the property owners. This can save millions of dollars in expenses from a city budget.

For these reasons, new PUDs are now far more readily approved by city planning and zoning commissions than non-planned developments. According to the U.S. Census Bureau, in 2023 81% of new single-family houses sold were part of a planned unit development. This is an increase from just 62% in 2009 with a steady increase throughout those 15 years. (Characteristics of New Housing, Data, 2024)

Like most everything else, regular and special assessments are bound to increase with inflation. Fees paid to a homeowners association management company, legal costs, insurance premiums, improvements, maintenance, materials, and labor costs will probably increase with the annual rate of inflation. Therefore, a property owner would be well served to budget for an increase in these annual dues.

The fact that this payment, along with the property taxes and hazard insurance, is not discretionary should not be overlooked. Even when a house is paid for in full and owned free and clear of any liens, these three expenses will almost always continue...and are likely to continue to increase almost every single year.

5. Maintenance and Improvements

When comparing the cost and arguably care-free position of renting shelter, be it an apartment, condo or house, versus the cost and responsibilities of owning, there are still many more items to consider. While some of these budgetary items may be discretionary, many are always or will eventually be necessary.

Just like an HOA or condo association has expenses for maintenance and must save for future expenses that undoubtedly will arise, a property owner is subject to many of the same demands. Naturally, these demands and costs will differ widely from one house to the next, by size, structure, soundness, age, location, state, climate, region, and many other factors. Common sense dictates that certain characteristics will play a big factor in current and future costs.

There are many metrics that exist to estimate these costs. Some are very flawed such as saving $1 per square foot each year which completely disregards inflation over a possible 30-year time horizon or longer. As an example, the average square footage of new construction houses has increased only slightly over the last two decades, from just over 2,200sf to just over 2,400sf, a difference of about 10%. Meanwhile, the Consumer Price Index for All Items [CPI] has risen 66%. This $1/sf idea implies that the maintenance budget would be $2,200 for the home bought 20 years ago might still be the same or maybe even $2,400 today. But adjusting for inflation, it would likely need to be more like $3,700 to $4,000.

A 10% rule suggests saving an amount equal to 10% of the mortgage principal and interest, property taxes and homeowners insurance payments. Consider that any $500,000 house might be financed at an interest rate of 2.5% or 10%, while property taxes might be 0.50% or 2.00%, and hazard insurance can range from 0.25% up to 1.75% depending upon the location. These variables result in a potential maintenance budget discrepancy between $2,100 to $6,800.

Realizing how vastly different these estimates are makes it tough to determine which might be best suited for any particular home or location. Better to over budget than fall short of cash needed.

The 1% rule of thumb considers that 1% of the house market value is adequate for maintenance expenses. This is probably a more dependable guideline. On a $500,000 house, $5,000 might be a proper budget. This will also take into consideration adjustments for inflation as house values typically trend higher than CPI. It will also disregard any aspect of financing that may change over the years.

Home warranties may offer a decent defense against repair costs in the early years of homeownership. These policies may cover a wide range of repairs and even replacement of appliances, plumbing, electrical and other home features. But any reliance on such a policy might be risky and caution is appropriate in that regard. They oftentimes are now paid for by home builders or home sellers as they are relatively inexpensive. They may offer only discounted services and less than expected coverage. They may limit replacement to items that are less than a certain age. For instance, a twenty-year-old home may have a dishwasher of the same age. But the warranty may only include appliances that are no more than ten years old. And the policies lapse, naturally, so choosing to extend the duration of the coverage may or not be worthwhile. Probably so, considering any new major appliance will start at about $1,000. Simply put, read the fine print...

What follows may not be a complete list as every house is different. It is an attempt to familiarize first-time home buyers with many common care and maintenance items that might otherwise be overlooked in a budget for household expenditures. Walking through a hardware store might also serve to open the mind to potential problems that homeowners must deal with on a regular or infrequent basis. Parts, tools and labor are the three components of maintenance and/or repair costs.

Some of these items may indeed seem silly to mention for the seasoned home buyer. However, many first-time home buyers stretch really far to meet the down payment and closing cost requirements on the day of the transaction. And then they are unprepared and overwhelmed by the moving costs and unexpected little things that add up quickly, like a few hundred dollars for a locksmith to rekey the doors.

Turning on the water might be next where a deposit is likely to be required. Most cities lump water service and garbage removal into the same bill. This may only amount to a hundred or so dollars each month unless it is summertime in Texas and you have to keep the grass from dying!

This brings up the matter of having an irrigation system. That may involve buying a shovel and digging a few holes to find where a leak is. The good news is that sprinkler heads are cheap and simple to replace. But if it is a main valve that needs replaced, it may cost over $2,000 to hire a plumber to fix it. Without fixing it, the water bill may double or triple.

But a plumber isn't always necessary. Fixing a running toilet is simple enough with clear instructions on the back of the replacement parts packaging. If left unattended, that running toilet and a leaky faucet may double the monthly water bill.

The gas and/or electric is another matter which will likely require a deposit to have those services turned on. It may be safest to have a plumber hook up a gas clothes dryer if not already present. More costs on day one.

Monthly gas and/or electric bills can differ greatly from month to month. It is generally possible to obtain the previous 12 months of utility usage in order to prepare for future bills. These bills might vary dramatically from one house to the next based on the size, age, craftmanship, insulation and quality of materials used to build the house, climate, thermostat settings, and state rates among other things. It is not uncommon to see these bills fluctuate by 300% from one season to the next. A $200 bill in the spring and fall may easily be $600 or more in the coldest and warmest months of the year.

The heating, ventilation, and air conditioning [HVAC] system of the house will have a large impact on the monthly gas and/or electric bill. Proper maintenance will help keep this cost relatively low. It is recommended to change the air filters on a quarterly basis. This could be another couple of hundred dollars per year. But that is nothing compared to the $5,000, $10,000 or higher cost to replace these systems when they completely fail.

Externally, there are other costs to consider that when left unmaintained may cause problems within the house. Bug and pest control are a real thing and can be very expensive. This work doesn't necessarily need to be completed by a expert. But the time, expense and exposure to chemical applications to prevent bug infestations must be considered. Professional prevention is not cheap at a cost approaching or exceeding $500 each year.

And certain measures should be taken to keep rodents outside especially during colder months when they are apt to seek warmer shelter. Hiring a professional to remove large rodents and prevent further unwelcome guests from finding a way into a warm attic can cost $1,000 or more, like everything else depending upon the size of the house and relative to local wages.

Tree trimming is often an overlooked part of this problem. Squirrels gain attic access by reaching roof lines that are encroached by tree branches. It is best to keep any trees that are close to the roof trimmed back enough to be out of squirrel jumping reach. Removing fallen trees, dead trees or general tree trimming can be an annual fall chore if you have spent a few hundred dollars on a decent gas chainsaw and are willing to take the risk of operating one. Or, you can spend about the same amount or more every year to have a professional do it for you. Planting larger shade trees further away from a house may be more appropriate than what landscapers tend to do.

Overhanging branches also drop leaves into gutters. These should be cleaned each fall after the leaves fall but before freezing weather. One of the most common and expensive mishaps is when this is left undone. A heavy snow fall will melt but when that water can't properly drain down the water spout, it may instead flow into the house. This may cause water damage on ceilings and walls leading to thousands of dollars in drywall replacement and painting.

With a ladder and no fear of heights, cleaning gutters is just another chore to be completed like stringing Christmas lights. While the latter may be optional and not cheap, the former is strongly recommended. It should be clear that prevention is better than procrastination. Ladders and icy roofs are bad for the back.

Rooves are something to pay particular attention to when budgeting, maintaining, and considering improving a house. Like nearly all appliances, HVAC units, water heaters and other household components, a roof may last less than ten or longer than thirty years. Like most of these other items, a water heater will continue to heat water until one day it doesn't. And it is a tough argument to make that there is a benefit to early replacement until that day comes.

A roof may be the exception to that soft rule. Arguably, more damage can come through the roof or more precisely through degraded roof shingles than damage that can be caused by the failure of the other aforementioned items. And although it is not advisable to ever sell real estate (see Part 3), a new roof will increase the market value and appeal of a house for sale like few other items.

Indeed, contrary to conventional wisdom, few things increase the value of house apart from actually increasing the livable square footage by adding an addition to a house. A new roof, new windows, and a pool are the common exceptions. The new roof and windows add value for the same reasons, they both are expected to do a better job of keeping out the elements and reducing the bill to heat and/or cool the house.

Adding a pool is another matter. It will add value but at the same time create an increased liability and therefore a higher homeowners insurance premium. It will also add yet another maintenance cost. It may not appeal to all potential buyers or renters.

As for other home improvements, a sound argument has been made to do those sooner rather than later. Many homeowners seek to remodel the kitchen and/or bathrooms just prior to putting a house on the market. The theory is that this will garner a higher value than not having completed the improvements. While this may be true in many instances, it is not always so. Timing is important. To obtain peak value, the taste of the potential buyer or renter would have to match the remodel. But any remodeling is obviously more likely to match the taste of the current owner. As the argument goes, quite frankly, don't live in a crummy house only to make it nice just before leaving. Live in a nicer house now and enjoy it for a while.

This advice follows through to the next section where choosing a house is discussed. Consider the debate between buying the worst house on the block or the nicest one...

6. Property Value

"Location, Location, Location" is the title of a British reality TV show featuring guests who are shopping for a house. It has been airing consecutively for nearly a quarter of a century. The words, "location, location, location," have been seen in print for nearly a century as well. Location is universally recognized as the most important determining factor of real estate value.

To create a proper foundation for the importance of this ideology is to first understand three elements of real estate that in some minds make it the most desirable of any investment. Real estate is limited, tangible, and productive.

Unlike printed money or stocks that can be diluted in value by creating more, the amount of land on this planet is a fixed quantity. Apart from lava flows sitting next to volcanoes and islands made of sand right beside the ocean, there is only so much surface space of inhabitable land on the planet. The supply of real estate is limited.

Unlike cryptocurrency digits or the notional amount of bonds in a trading account, real estate is something you can physically touch. You can pick up the dirt and hold it in your hand. You can stand on it, step on it, jump on it, and it isn't going anywhere. The land of real estate is tangible.

And unlike fine art or jewelry, real estate has the potential of eternal productive value. Real estate typically includes the surface area, and also the land below all the way to the core of the earth and the sky above into the heavens. Imagine the opportunities. The theoretical value of any parcel of land includes the natural resources of minerals, water, game and timber, the potential agricultural productivity of cultivating crops or raising animals, and the residential and commercial possibilities from a campsite to a commercial high-rise building. While its best current use may demand a current market value, that can change from generation to generation. Real estate may become more or less productive but will almost always retain some utility value.

a. Land

Recall that property tax has two components, the land and its improvements. The facts that land is limited, tangible, and productive is why real estate is assessed a separate value for its lot size by square feet or acres. Otherwise, a vacant quarter acre lot in the middle of Manhattan, New York, would hold the exact same value as the same size lot in Manhattan, Montana. And those land values are simply not equal.

Real estate's current best productive use is what makes its location the most critical element. For residential real estate, the inherent value is determined by several factors. The most important might be considered environment, education and employment.

Environment rightly boils down to safety because staying alive trumps all. Access to healthcare and distance to hospitals are pretty important to everyone. This can be taken to the extreme to prove the point. While living on a deserted island has a certain appeal, living next to the Mayo Clinic in Rochester, Minnesota, would be more advantageous if it weren't for the cold of winter. Similarly, distance from a fire department is taken into consideration to determine eligibility for some loan programs.

Crime is also a component of environment. And there are numerous statistics for every local that convey the safety of living in any particular state, county, city and neighborhood which should be considered to have an effect on the value of the land. Even the little things like a well-lit street at night, proper sidewalks, or a house situated on a cul-de-sac will increase the value from one street or neighborhood to the next. As expressed earlier, gated communities offer value well above non-gated communities for the added safety it represents.

Education is perhaps the next most important factor with consideration to residential land value. School ratings are clearly broadcast with every house listing and maybe a top priority for homebuyers or renters with school age children or those planning for them one day. Ample daycare options will present additional value.

Being near the campus of a college or university has benefits, too, that may often be overlooked. In addition to the access for education to further one's career, they may offer high quality libraries, museums, performing arts and athletic events for cultural experiences and entertainment value. Their faculty and students may also turn out to be a valuable rental market. Educational opportunities add value. Consider the difference between Manhattan, Kansas, home of Kansas State University versus Manhattan, Nevada, with a population of 124.

Employment opportunities are also fundamental to area land value. The United States has always made available the opportunity for its citizens to migrate from one state to another with little if any restriction. This mobility to seek employment opportunities raises values where employment levels are above average for sustained periods of time. For instance, Florida and Texas have had lower than average unemployment rates since the turn of the century. And property prices have increased accordingly due to a strong demand for housing.

Certain cities and states have immense economic development platforms that make overt efforts to woo corporations with tax incentives to move operations or build out operations in their area. Jobs bring in residents. Residents pay property taxes used to improve the community. It might be a vicious cycle, but those residents obtain a higher quality of life and have a job so, most importantly, they are able to pay for their shelter.

Clearly the opposite has been true for once thriving manufacturing powerhouses like Detroit and Pittsburgh. High rates of unemployment decrease land values as homeowners are less likely to be able to meet the costs of homeownership or even pay rent.

More locally, there are other considerations of convenience that may imply more or less value. Convenience may tie into environment, education, and employment, too. In an ideal world for a city dweller, if the general practitioner, hospital, police station, fire department, daycare, private school, drycleaner, grocer, and plenty of restaurants are all a short block or two away from a townhouse or brownstone, while the office, university and airport are just a short cab or subway ride away, the only real decision to be made is which side of Central Park one might prefer.

Commuting distances is at the forefront of convenience. Some of these conveniences may be more important than others and increase expenses of discretionary spending to the extent of straining housing affordability. Mass transit, toll roads, all the way down to paved roads have an intrinsic value on real estate. Food deserts are described as where the nearest grocery store is more than a mile away for at least a third of the population. But urban, suburban and rural communities have relatively different notions of convenience. Yet this difference between densities of population and distance to necessities has a direct correlation to land value.

Location is also specific to each lot. As mentioned before, a house that sits on a cul-de-sac or one on a corner lot will trade at a premium to a house that is not. This becomes obvious when considering a beachfront estate. A house with a skyline, water or golf course view, as examples, will fetch a much higher price than any without. But keep in mind some of those views may not be protected. A window with a picturesque view may one day face a wind turbine, smoke stack or highway.

The long-term value of land is not assured. Municipal decisions to permit any future development of adjacent or non-adjacent land may have a huge impact on a property's long-term land value. Once this is understood, then further consideration might also be applied to the future improvement or decay of the environment, better or worse educational opportunities, and growth or shrinkage of employment, which all may largely be dependent on local and state management of resources.

To be clear, county property taxes assessments are broken into two parts of land and improvements, as previously stated. And that assessed value is not necessarily the market value. Yet, residential real estate markets rarely make this distinction of value between land and improvements.

Gentrification of neighborhoods portrays a reason why market value should be evaluated by both terms. Gentrification of a neighborhood is the term used to describe one instance that land usage might change from generation to generation, through shorter or longer periods of time. The term is derived from the word "gentry." In a class structure, this would follow royalty and nobility, to include an upper class of landowners thus ranking by wealth and social status above the peasant class. So, gentrification as used in real estate markets is a neighborhood which is becoming inhabited by more prosperous owners or renters.

With the increased purchasing power of the gentry, or just anyone with an income or wealth higher than the average for that street, neighborhoods can experience a transformation. This generally might begin with just one house on which increased discretionary spending is applied to better maintenance and landscaping. It could continue to include exterior improvements like a fresh coat of paint or new siding, new fencing or a new roof. Money spent on these items improves curb appeal.

Just this one house with better curb appeal may attract a buyer to a neighboring house for sale. And then that buyer makes similar improvements inducing a snowball effect where over time, most or all of the homes on the street have an improved appearance and thus lifting the market value of the transformed neighborhood. The higher purchase prices extract higher property taxes which if used efficiently will improve municipal amenities and schools.

But it may not end there. Enter the tear downs. Eventually the localized environment, education and employment opportunities are so sought after that even more affluent buyers are attracted to a specific neighborhood. But the houses available may be too small or old for their tastes. So a property is bought at market value; however, the house is knocked down, and a larger, shiny, new house is erected in its place. In this scenario, although full market value inclusive of its improvement value may have been paid, the new owner bought the property purely for its perceived land value. And in practice, the new house may be worth more when completed than the land purchase, demolition and new construction costs.

This is the same strategy used by land developers. They may buy farmland for fair market value of its current agricultural use but repurpose the land for a housing development. The infusion of cash to make an improvement, improve the improvement, or replace an aged improvement with a new improvement may all add value to the land component or underlying and surrounding real estate.

The opposite of gentrification can also occur. A city or town may be thriving and thus have elevated property prices today. But the factors that contribute to the demand of living in that area may change. This might happen over decades or even overnight. This would most often be attributed to an economic change such as lost job opportunities. A factory may shut down. A corporation's headquarters may relocate. A new housing development or attraction may lure money further away.

There are numerous examples that could be cited. What was once "the steel belt" is now "the rust belt" as the auto industry moved manufacturing away from the Midwest and Northeast. More recently, the ability and acceptance to work from home has accelerated a shift from suburban to rural living. These types of socio-economic changes may be hard to predict but they are also hard to overlook. Although it is not always necessary to value the land and its improvements separately, the notion that they may change are important to understand.

b. Improvements

The second component of residential property value is the improvement or dwelling that is the condo, co-op, or house along with any additional structures and/or amenities.

The most common residential dwelling is a single-family residence [SFR] that stands by itself on a parcel of land. This is known as being detached as opposed to attached. Any dwelling that shares one or more common walls is considered attached, such as a townhome.

The label of a condo, co-op, apartment, townhome, or any other name is determined initially by the developer and how they had or have decided to describe it to the county for approval or permit. This label may have consequences to financing and insuring the property, among other issues.

Residential real estate is limited by the number of "units" that are attributed to the property according to the county property tax records. For instance, a single-family unit in condominium project, co-operative or apartment building would be residential property and each unit would be taxed separately. Up to four units on the same property tax bill would also be considered residential property. This would include a duplex or triplex.

Therefore, any property sold that has five separate dwelling units or more is considered a multi-family, commercial property. Any property that has both a residential dwelling combined with space used for a business purpose, more than just a home office, is also considered a mixed-use, commercial property. This usually would include even the appearance of a business purpose, from a barber's chair in a den to commercial-grade kitchen in a garage. Or it could be a rowhouse with a retail shop on the first floor and a living space on the second floor.

What might be considered a practical renovation to make use of unused living space in order to run a business may become extremely problematic when trying to sell or refinance a house. Mixed-use properties typically will require unconventional, commercial financing that is typically much more expensive than residential financing.

Even condominium projects are limited to the percentage of space allocated to retail or commercial space, such as the street level floors of a building in an urban setting. Most developers are usually keenly aware of such limitations where novice developers may make costly mistakes.

Single-family residences can also be limited by other factors that may create problems for financing. These problems usually arise when an appraisal is requested or completed. This will be discussed in detail later, but similar residences must exist in order to properly complete an appraisal.

For instance, a renovation may include adapting part of the home into what is referred to as a mother-in-law suite. This may or may not have a separate entrance or a kitchenette. It may be quite sufficient for a mother-in-law, or as a rental unit within a home. Basements, attics, or a separate building, like a pool house, may be useful for guests or even to rent. These are called accessory dwelling units [ADUs] when they have utilities that can be billed or metered separately from the main house or main dwelling unit. For most lending purpose, there may be no more than two accessory dwelling units on a property.

Too many other additional structures may also become a source of frustration for homeowners. Multiple barns, sheds, or other outbuildings may raise red flags that a property is used as a working farm or has agricultural value that is uncommon for the area. This form of mixed-use, where agricultural income is generated from the property, typically does not conform to residential real estate lending standards.

These types of improvements, renovations or additions are very common in certain markets but not all. Regardless of whether permits for the work are either obtained or even required, an appraiser must be able to find other properties by which to form an opinion of the value of these improvements. If unable to do so, financing options become scarce if available at all.

The structure and building materials of a home may also pose problems for appraisers and, therefore, conventional financing. Log cabins, dome structures, and barndominiums are a few examples that may be problematic in some areas of the country but not others.

Manufactured homes that are pre-built off-site and pieced together on the property can be difficult to finance. Mobile homes are less readily financed as they must meet very specific guidelines. A specialty lender might be more familiar and capable of handling such transactions. It should be noted on a parcel of land where a single-family residence is situated, a mobile home is not considered an accessory dwelling unit. This structure would likely need to be removed from the land in order to refinance or enable a buyer to finance the purchase of the property. This would be true and especially difficult when the mobile home is affixed to the ground in the normal manner.

While it may sound to some like a good idea to buy a house on several acres and add a row of mobile homes to rent out, it is probably unwise to do so. Although this endeavor could generate decent income in the near term, converting a residential property into a small commercial mobile home park would ultimately diminish the value of the property simply because there are far fewer people that would be able to buy the property as conventional financing would be off the table.

As lending guidelines change from time to time, it may be wise to speak a lender prior to investing money that materially changes the nature of the house or property. What may very well be added value in terms of commercial or rental income may turn out to decrease the value of the property if potential buyers are unable to obtain normal financing.

What is undeniably true with residential real estate is that one can generally never go wrong with a traditional three-bedroom, two-bathroom house with some curb appeal. This would be considered a typical starter home. As opposed to a non-traditional house as described above, the demand for a normal house of this size will exceed all others simply on the basis of housing affordability.

> *"Wall Street housing investors tend to herd into the same neighborhoods because their algorithms spot the same opportunities. They screen the country for cities and towns with population growth and job openings – places where there is likely to be competition for homes. They prefer to own three-bedroom, suburban properties that are around 1,500 square feet in size and offer a convenient commute to downtown. Young parents like these kinds of homes, and landlords like to rent to families because they become sticky tenants once their children enroll in local schools."*
>
> (Ryan, 2024)

The luxury of a larger house with more bedrooms and bathrooms is great and obviously necessary for large families. Houses are primarily valued according to livable square footage. The larger the home, the more costly.

Therefore, a home that is affordable and suitable to the largest percentage of the population will arguably have the most ordinal utility. Whereas a home with more bedrooms than might be required for the average family size and less affordable for the average household income will only add marginal utility and thus diminishing value per square foot.

That isn't to say that there is not a market for enormous luxury homes. It is purely a direct statement regarding the more practical application of residential housing dollars. The cost of insurance, taxes, and maintenance of mansions, chateaus, estates and the like are proportionately higher. The liquidity is far less as the market for buyers is fewer as is the market for renters. And because of this, the price volatility is exponentially greater though admittedly both ways, up and down. If the right buyer comes along and loves the place, top dollar will be paid. True too is that the higher the value, the higher percentage the price may fall by a motivated, multi-millionaire seller.

7. Real Estate Agent Commission

Prior to looking at homes on the internet, visiting some open houses, or contacting a realtor, what should first be done is to contact a mortgage lender. Many people get this backwards, putting the cart before the horse.

A mortgage lender will first determine a borrower's eligibility to obtain financing, discuss the purchasing power available to buy a house, and provide a pre-approval letter for a loan amount within that range. This amount may not and probably should not be the maximum that may be obtainable. To the contrary, this amount should be more in line with what a borrower can easily afford.

Talking with a good lender first will help avoid a borrower to, "...think that they must have such a one as their neighbors have," Thoreau's quote from page one.

Talking to a real estate agent first is a mistake. Not because they are bad, but because their job is to show each client a house they will fall in love with in order to sell them that house. An experienced realtor will want to avoid showing a house the customer cannot afford. They will likely require a pre-approval letter prior in order to show houses within the customer's price range.

But just as it is typically true that a mortgage lender's commission is a percentage of the size of the loan, so too is the real estate agents' commissions. Each is incentivized contrary to what might be in their customers' best interest. A lender gets paid more if the loan amount is larger. A real estate buyer's agent gets paid more if the sales price is higher. It is deceitful to represent that either may be wholly negotiating in the customer's best interest when their income is adversely affected by doing so.

Of course, the same could be said about a waiter who only recommends the priciest dish on the menu. Their tip is likely based on a percentage of the total bill. And, therefore, it is beneficial for the check to be bigger. This doesn't make the waiter or waitress a bad person, nor the loan originator or the real estate agent. But it would be a bit naïve to think that their financial interest is always one hundred percent aligned with their customer's financial interest.

Real estate agents can be extremely knowledgeable, useful and often a necessary part of the buying and selling process. This is demonstrated by the difficulty to obtain a real estate agent. Texas currently leads the way in the burden of requirements to get licensed by requiring 180 hours of pre-licensure coursework. Most state require anywhere from 60 to 120 hours with a handful only mandating as few as 40 hours of class room time. Passing a state exam is required in all states before practicing. And that is usually followed by some degree of post-licensure education and continuing education every one, two or three years depending on the state.

Most of this course work is concerned with contract law, real estate law, owner's rights as well as the process and common issues that arise in real estate transactions. Like most professionals, real estate agents are relied upon to provide insight and expertise that is often gained mostly by experience more so than class time. For first time home buyers especially, relying upon a seasoned real estate agent who has years of practice and hundreds of transactions is perhaps more prudent than giving a shot to a friend or relative who has recently entered the field.

According to the National Association of REALTORS®, they had over 1.5 million members in 2024. Membership is required in order to be distinguished from a simple agent. Nearly all licensed real estate agents elect to obtain the REALTOR® designation and renew their membership annually.

Over the last few decades approximately four to five million new and existing homes are sold on average each year. With an agent on each side of the table for the buyer and the seller, that means about ten million agent transactions annually, or only six to seven deals for every agent each year.

However, those agents with more than six years of experience accounted for approximately 70% of transactions nationwide, with a median of 12 transactions per agent. This was three times more than those with three to five years of experience while those with two years or less of experience had carried only about 5% of total transactions. (National Association of REALTORS Research Group, 2024) The disparity of transaction counts between more versus less experienced agents reinforces the notion that a seasoned agent has abundantly more knowledge to guide a client through their first or second purchase or sale.

For instance, an agent with many years of experience and transactions under their belt may have more local knowledge about the various neighborhoods, schools, and similar home sales in the market. More importantly, they have probably witnessed different types of transactions, tactics, work arounds, fixes, and overcome a multitude of other pitfalls that may torpedo a transaction and be able to utilize that skill set to avoid similar issues in the next transaction. The same could be said about working with an experienced mortgage loan originator. Theoretical situations contained in academic learning environments is often inferior to real world, hands-on experience held by an industry veteran.

Homeowners engage a real estate agent to sell their house. They might interview several to see who they may be most comfortable working with and who may be the most competent and able to complete the transaction. A real estate agent representing the seller provides a host of services in this arrangement. Many of these services may be overlooked by a home listed for sale by owner, FSBO in industry lingo. And some are only able to be provided by a licensed agent.

For instance, only real estate agents have access to the area's Multiple Listing Service or MLS. Through the MLS, they are able to look at the most recent home sales in order to ascertain an appropriate asking price for the house. They are likely to know better at what price the house may sell, more so than a biased homeowner who appreciates the value for the effort and care they may have put into the home as well as sentimental value. But a good real estate agent would likely disregard this value as would potential buyers.

Initially listing a house above fair market value is a good way to ultimately get far less. The more days a home is on the market, the less chance it will sell at asking price. Potential buyers will, fairly or not, assume it has gone unsold because it is either overpriced or there is something unappealing about it so they may choose not to bother taking a closer look. An appropriate initial price is a key factor in selling a house at fair market value.

Only real estate agents can list a house for sale on MLS. That listing on the MLS is where other real estate websites are able to compile the information available to the public to browse the internet for houses. Without a home listed on MLS through a real estate agent, the exposure to reach potential buyers is severely diminished.

A seller's agent may also advise the owner of certain quick improvements that could be done in order to achieve the highest fair market value. A fresh coat of paint in certain rooms, reducing some clutter, something as simple as a few air fresheners, or more involved like staging a house with newer furniture can elicit more offers. And a professional who regularly visits homes with client buyers and gains their feedback will notice the potential that a house has that would be overlooked by the current owner. An open house must show well or it will provide lackluster results.

The selling agent will also use their network of colleagues to expose, gain interest and solicit offers from other buyer agents' customers. And those offers are when the negotiating begins and the real value of an experienced agent helps the most.

Many factors will determine when it might be best to accept the first offer received, counter-offer, or be patient for a better offer to come along. Real estate market data and trends plays a big role in these decisions.

Supply and demand are at the heart of the data. A real estate agent will know the empirical data that all are privy to but is almost always dated. And they will also understand more current and relevant anecdotal info heard on the street.

Perhaps the most important relevant data point is the months of inventory or housing stock. Six months of supply of homes for sale is considered normal. This indicates that there are six times the average number of homes sold per month.

If one house is sold per month in a town, then six houses currently listed for sale would be six months of supply. If there are only two or three homes listed for sale, then supply would be considered tight. In this case, there is a likelihood that a better offer may be received and patience may be advisable. This would be a seller's market. On the other hand, if there are a dozen houses listed for sale, an entire year of supply, then any reasonable offer would be worth entertaining. This would be a buyers' market because they have the upper hand. They have more choices available to them than in a normal market.

A real estate agent's insight is helpful. Perhaps they know there are two more houses that are soon to be listed or two houses that are soon to be under contract. This information would change the calculation and bargaining power of both the buyer and the seller, but only if they also are aware of the pending situation.

It is also no secret that the time of year plays a role in the prospect of selling a house. Families with school aged children are naturally reluctant to move during the course of the school year from one school district to another. So, more homes are listed for sale in the spring. Counterintuitively, this means supply is lower in the fall and winter, but then again, there are also fewer buyers.

Local home price trends are also important. And this may be subject to non-real estate specific information such as if a company has decided to expand operations or move their headquarters into town. This would obviously have the potential to drive up home prices in which case waiting for a better offer, if timing is not a concern, may be advisable. Of course, the opposite is once again true, too. A good realtor may be aware of these factors more so than the average person focused on their own profession and family.

Once a price is agreed upon, the details of a contract are formalized between the parties. Standardization of contracts are typically set by each state and their real estate regulatory body. These are usually boiler plate purchase and sale agreements where the specific details are limited to fill-in-the-blank spaces. By and large, residential real estate transactions tend to be materially consistent with few if any alterations to the form contract provided by the property state. That is to say, within each state, the same form is used. And with similar frameworks of law, although they are written differently it could be said they all read the same from state to state.

Real estate agents continue to be involved in coordination of vendors that belong in each transaction until the final closing when the sale is consummated. Real estate agents get paid from the proceeds of the transaction. And they get paid well.

When listing a house for sale with a real estate agent, the seller historically has agreed to pay their agent a commission for the services listed above. The seller's agent normally cedes half the commission to the buyer's agent for their part in selling the house to their client, the buyer.

Each real estate agent is typically employed by a real estate broker, the person or firm that maintains the licenses and other necessities required to operate the business of transacting in real estate. Therefore, the commission, as much as 6%, is normally split equally four ways between the seller's agent and their boss, the selling brokerage, and the buyer's agent and their boss, the buying brokerage.

Historically, real estate agents were able to represent both the seller and buyer in the same transaction. Of late, this entire arrangement has come under scrutiny. As a buyer might now engage a real estate agent to represent and solicit an offer on their behalf for less than a standard amount, that buyer's agent is still incentivized by a higher sales price. As alluded to earlier, it is and always has been dubious to negotiate on behalf of the buyer for the lowest price while being paid by the seller who desires the highest price. And most sellers probably won't consider their reduced transaction cost as a reason to lower the sales price by an equal amount.

The seemingly obvious solution but least likely to materialize is a fee-based structure for the buyer's agent rather than a percentage-based commission. But a "buyer" might just be a shopper who wants to be brought around to look inside dozens of homes but then are under no obligation to ever transact. The quality of representation would arguably diminish under this type of arrangement as buyer's agents would be reluctant to commit their time without a proper incentive. And that creates a problem for the prospective buyer who may fully intend to buy and commit to pay a commensurate fee but doesn't find an appealing home or whose situation changes. Yet they still must pay the agent a fee for their time. It is a conundrum where sellers are advantaged.

8. Inspection

When a sales price has been agreed upon and the purchase contract has been signed by both the buyer and seller, an earnest money deposit is required to be provided, usually within three days. As the name implies, this check is to provide the seller with confidence of the buyer's intention to complete the transaction. In turn, the seller is obligated to not entertain other offers showing their intention to the buyer to deal fairly and honor the contract.

The earnest money amount is not the proposed down payment, but a smaller sum typically of a few thousand dollars. This check is made out to the title company or wired to them and held in an escrow or trust account until the transaction is completed. The amount is applied as a credit or partial payment toward the purchase at the closing.

The earnest money is eligible to be returned to the buyer under certain circumstances stipulated in the purchase contract. For instance, there is almost always a mortgage clause that states that if a borrow is unable to obtain the necessary financing, then the contract is voided and the title company will release the earnest money from the escrow account and return it to the buyer.

Prior to that, as one of the first items to be completed after the contract is signed, is the inspection. There is generally a time frame within two weeks when this should be completed. To be clear, the inspection and the appraisal are two entirely different things. The appraisal is an objective determination of value from an uninterested third party used in conjunction with financing. A home inspection is an assessment of the condition of the house and its components, not value.

It is highly recommended to have a home inspection completed by a reputable company. Although it is not even a requirement to have a home inspection, it is certainly worthwhile. The primary goal of the inspection is to determine that everything in the house is functioning as intended and not on the verge of collapse or in need of imminent repair at great expense. At the very least, it is to make sure the home is in livable state. It is like a certificate of occupancy, an approval on a newly constructed home where a final inspection would be completed by a municipal employee.

This type of inspection is supposed to be a completely thorough examination and report of every aspect of the home from top to bottom, inside and out. It is useful first to determine if the house has been maintained properly, is in generally good working condition, without any major defects, and is suitable to proceed with the purchase. This should not be misunderstood to expect a report that everything about the house is in perfect condition. In actuality, even a brand-new house often has minor flaws and items that just aren't right, maybe some light switches were installed in an odd place.

The secondary benefit of a home inspection is to provide an expectation for what lies ahead. In many ways a home inspection can be compared to the reserve study that homeowners and condo associations are required to complete every five years in order to assess and budget for expected maintenance and repairs on the communal property. It will likely point out some wear and tear or recommend items that could be fixed or replaced to improve efficiency or prevent further deterioration of dependent components. But these items may be more suggestions and not necessarily be an unnecessary condition to impose on the seller prior to completing the purchase. It will also contain valuable information to provide a road map for maintenance such as when to replace air filters or when to flush out the water in an older gas furnace.

With a new or existing house, not everything will be perfect or last forever. An inspection will detail the expected remaining life of systems and appliances in order to prepare for those expenses as detailed in the previous chapter on maintenance.

However, there may be elements that ought to be fixed prior to an appraisal or prior to completing the purchase. Sometimes, these are items that the seller may have been unaware of themselves. And they might very well be compelled to pay for to fix in order to complete the sale. Without doing so, the next potential buyer would likely uncover the recurring issue with their inspection. Reviewing the inspection with the inspector and then with the real estate agent to understand these needs and remedies is to be expected.

As a condition for lending, The Department of Veterans Affairs [VA] requires a separate inspection for termite infestation in all but a few states. They also require any home that depends on a well as a water source to have the water tested for contaminants. But they do not require the actual pump and plumbing leading into the house be inspected as a condition for lending. However, it is items of this nature that might warrant a certified inspector to have a look at to make sure it is in good working condition. Consider that if the VA requires a termite inspection in that state, it may be prudent to have one completed whether a lender requires it or not.

By no means is the following meant to portray a comprehensive list of items that ought to be inspected. Rather, it is an incomplete short list intended to give a general idea of some of the major elements that would typically be evaluated. Any number of home inspection company websites will provide greater detail of these items. It would be wise to compare the lists from several local, certified companies before choosing one to complete the job.

In doing so, a buyer may find additional items outside of the usual and customary list that ought to be inspected on the particular house they are purchasing. A house with a pool should probably have the water pumps and filtration systems checked, as an example.

Exterior: roof, attic, insulation, crawlspaces, gutters, irrigation & drainage

Plumbing: water heater, pipes, sinks, tubs, showers, toilets, septic system

Electrical: lighting, switches, outlets, breakers, wiring, fans, fire alarms & smoke detectors

Temperature Control: furnace, heating, ventilation, air conditioning, fireplace, chimney, thermostat

Structural: foundation, walls, windows, doors, locks, concrete driveways & sidewalks

Appliances: stove, oven, refrigerator, trash compactor, garbage disposal, washer, dryer

Infestation: mold, rodents, bugs, & termites

9. Appraisal

A market value appraisal is an estimated price of property based on the most recent sales of the most similar homes nearest the subject property. These three parameters, recent, similar, and near, are the fundamental basis of a residential real estate appraisal.

The value of each of these houses is then adjusted to match the subject property to provide an average price per square foot. That price is then multiplied by the total square feet of the subject property to compute a market value.

Several factors may warrant the disparity between the houses used as comparisons. The fewer homes that have traded in recent months, the uniqueness of the subject property, and density of houses in any area will provide leeway in which an appraiser is able to locate and choose comparable properties. The determination to consider other properties as relevant which are outside of the normal parameters for time since its sale, size, and distance is what make appraisals somewhat subjective. An appraisal is only one person's opinion of value at a certain moment in time.

Generally speaking, houses that are used as comparable properties will have sold within the past one to three months. The more recent the better. But when a house is unique or sales are sporadic, it may prove necessary to use a house or two sold further back but within the past year. Any property sold more than a year ago is doubtful to be used in an appraisal. Likewise, an adjacent house of equal size that might be listed for sale will not be considered in an appraisal.

An appraiser is obligated to the best of their ability and judgement to try to find at least three similar sized houses with one that is only slightly smaller, one about the same size, and one slightly larger in livable square footage. The difference in the comparable square footage may vary from one appraisal to the next but are likely to be within 10-20% of the same size.

These similar homes should have the same basic characteristics of the subject property. When the subject property is a ranch-style, single story house then the comparable properties should also be ranch-style, single story houses. If the subject property is on a two-acre lot, then so too should be the relative properties. In the same sense, the neighborhoods should be fundamentally similar. For instance, a fifty-year-old house in a gentrified neighborhood would not have a comparable property listed that is in a new development even though it sold last month and is less than a half mile away.

Of course, the comparable properties aren't expected to be identical. For each instance the appraiser will adjust the line item by a dollar amount. As an example, maybe one comparable house has no pool but the subject property does. The comparable property will be increased in value by an amount representative of the cost of the pool, perhaps an addition of twenty thousand dollars to its actual previous sales price. Certain other pricing adjustments may be made at the discretion of the appraiser, like the value of a new versus aged roof.

Bear in mind that both of these examples are external features. It is likely not known by the appraiser if one of the comparable houses had an old, outdated or well-worn original kitchen from when the house was built twenty-five years ago. They do not have access to other appraisals as it is the sole property of the person that paid for it. An appraiser only has access to the interior of the subject property. While it may be true that a house with an updated kitchen sells for more, this adjustment in value may not always be supported by the appraisal. A notation to that effect would be included in the appraisal report according to the standard definitions found in the Uniform Appraisal Dataset [UAD] (see Appendix A). (Selling Guide, 2024)

Similarly, the property condition and quality are categorized as per the UAD guidelines. Houses that are rated C6 or Q6 are generally not eligible for financing until the specifically mentioned repairs are completed. These are likely to be first found by a home inspection but not always. And again, these repairs would usually be at the expense of the current owner. In these instances, an additional appraisal charge will often be required to have an appraiser return and verify the repair requirements have been satisfied.

In addition to the indication of market value, appraisals have a cost approach analysis. This estimates the labor and material total dollars that would be required to rebuild the house in the same form. It is generally in-line with the market value.

Residential property appraisals are highly consistent in nearly all respects as the standard is set and maintained by the Federal Housing Finance Agency [FHFA]. The Uniform Residential Appraisal Report has been adopted by most all residential lenders. It requires specific details, criteria and data points to be recorded that is an attempt to include all relevant information that can be defined, categorized, and compared from one dwelling to another. By doing so and adopting additional standard reporting requirements, the financing market is moving toward utilizing asset valuation models [AVMs]. Asset valuation models utilize this information to categorize homogenous properties and estimate their value in local markets.

The availability and acceptable tolerance for price accuracy of these tools has allowed lenders to use them as an alternative for requiring a full appraisal in many purchase and refinance transactions. Where an appraisal will normally cost a borrower $500 to $1,000, an appraisal waiver reliant on an internally adopted asset valuation model will cost nothing, saving both money and time.

This makes sense in more ways than one. On refinance transactions, an appraisal waiver is usually provided only by the current holder of the mortgage. As they already have a claim and working knowledge of the asset including a record of the previous appraisal, it is not an added element of risk for them to refinance the same property. With regard to purchases, it is surprising how often the appraisal is returned with a value equal to or just a few thousand dollars above the purchase contract amount. When the buyer is providing sufficient equity to marginalize the rare price discrepancy revealed by an appraisal, then risk is mitigated and the value of an appraisal is de minimis.

On the other hand, some transactions require duplicate appraisals and/or supplemental estimates provided in addition to the traditional appraisal. Oftentimes, lenders will require two appraisals for houses valued above a certain amount. This threshold was previously and may remain $1 million at the discretion of the lender.

Houses financed as investment properties require a "Single-Family Comparable Rent Schedule" which may cost an additional several hundred dollars. As the name denotes, this addendum indicates the monthly rental income that a property would be expected to receive. This rent schedule may be designated for long-term or short-term rental but not both. The rent estimate is valuable information for investors but can also be an important data point even for a buyer who intends to live in the house as their primary residence. More about this can be found in the Chapter 18 regarding the Debt Service Coverage Ratio.

It is also important to first know what loan program (see Chapter 22. The Secondary Market and Mortgage Insurance) is intended to be used as certain programs require additional parameters when ordering the appraisal. As an example, with regard to a loan insured through the Department of Veteran's Affairs program, a VA loan, the appraisal must be ordered by the lender directly on the VA portal. This will be completed by an appraiser with a special VA certification.

An FHA loan requires similar caution as these appraisals are also slightly more exhaustive, requiring certain items like handrails on staircases beyond a certain number of steps. An FHA appraisal can typically be adjusted to be used for a conventional loan program for a fee charged by the appraiser. However, the opposite may not be true as it is not a two-way street. An entirely new FHA appraisal might be necessary if a consumer does not ultimately qualify for a normal, conforming loan, but instead has to resort to an FHA loan.

An appraisal is always to be ordered by the lender who will engage an appraisal management company to hire a local appraiser within their network willing to complete the request. Despite the lender choosing the appraisal management company, the borrower pays for the appraisal.

On a purchase, the appraiser will normally contact the seller's agent to arrange for access into the house. On a refinance, the appraiser will contact the homeowner directly.

Because this is supposed to be an independent estimate of value, it is sound advice to refrain from engaging with the appraiser other than answering any questions they may have. It is not uncommon to have an appraisal come in below an expected value and learn that the homeowner was eager to convey the finer points of a home's worth from their point of view. A tidy house and passive interaction will likely do best.

The appraisal report is to be provided to the consumer upon receipt by the lender or at least three days prior to completing the transaction. This should be reviewed for omissions and errors as sometimes appraisers make mistakes although it is highly uncommon. If a material error is found, like the square footage is clearly wrong, then the lender may try to correct the issue through the appraisal management company. But, in order to maintain impartiality, they are forbidden by federal regulations to communicate any grievances with regard to value or nonmaterial differences. However, the consumer has every right to convey these complaints and demonstrate substantive reasons for reconsideration directly to the appraiser in their effort to increase the noted value.

A good example of when this may be appropriate is if there are comparable properties that maybe should have been considered but the appraiser, for some reason, was not aware or chose not to use them. It is reasonable to acknowledge that a homeowner could be more familiar with local neighborhood transactions more so than an appraiser who might be unfamiliar with that particular market, most especially in larger cities or metropolitan areas. However, the appraiser may have had very specific reasons for not using those exact properties in their report. It certainly may be worth a phone call to the appraiser but only if it will have an impact on the transaction.

Generally speaking, appraisals that are ordered by the lender through an appraisal management company and completed by a certified appraiser are eligible to be transferred to another lender. However, many lenders balk at the idea and may refuse to do so suggesting their internal policy. Arguably, this is an effort to contain borrowers who have already consumed some amount of the lender's time and effort to endeavor in providing the loan for profit. On the other hand, the borrower is the one that paid for the appraisal and it is rightfully theirs. If requested, it is a bit ignoble to not release to the borrower the three distinct files that together constitute the appraisal. But some lenders will only provide the PDF copy as required by law. This is especially true when that same lender is more than willing to accept an appraisal that was initiated by a competitor. As such, it may be a proper question to ask each lender up front prior to paying for an appraisal from them.

Appraisals have a shelf life of 90 days. Beyond that time frame, most lenders will require a new appraisal. Although, in rare circumstances and up to the discretion of the lender, a recertification by the same appraiser may be acceptable but only within a very short time frame beyond that 90-day window from the completion date, perhaps a few days at most.

10.   Title Insurance and Fees

Title is a right to ownership, in this case, of residential real estate. A deed is the document that formalizes this right of ownership. When real estate ownership is transferred from one person to another, a new deed is created as a formal document signed by the current owner declaring the transference of their ownership right to the new owner. This deed is then filed with the county clerk's office to serve as a permanent record of this assignment.

However, there may be other claims to entitlement of the property that may have previously existed and surface throughout the course of time unbeknownst to the buyer. When financing a residential property, a lender's title insurance will always be required. This protects the lender from monetary losses against such defects in the clean transfer of title. This insurance policy remains in effect until the loan is paid in full and a lien release is issued to the owner. Unfortunately, this insurance policy does not transfer from one loan or lender to the next which would considerably reduce the cost of a refinance transaction.

The cost of a lender's loan title policy is different from state to state. A majority of states set the allowable rate, others approve the cost that each title company might publish for policies produced on properties within that state, and a handful do not determine or regulate the costs. Typically, the cost, regardless of state, in some form or another is a function of the purchase price, usually from 0.3% to as much as 1.5%, along with a standard or excess fixed amount. Other adjustments may also be made, such as in Texas where the premium amount of a refinance policy is discounted based on the date of issuance of the prior loan's title insurance policy.

Where the cost of a policy is not a formula pre-determined by a state regulator it would be wise to shop around for a title insurance company that offers a reasonable rate. It is not uncommon in purchase transactions for the seller to provide and pay for the title insurance policy. And so, it is they who decide which title company will be used. In a refinance transaction, the owner has the right to choose the title insurance company.

An owner's title insurance policy is optional for the borrower when financing or paying cash, and is highly recommended for the same benefits. An owner's policy may last for the duration of homeownership until the title-holder legally transfers the property. It is relatively cheap, often a mere $100, when purchased in conjunction with a lender's policy.

There are numerous common issues where a clean title was not conveyed to the buyer and which justify the high cost of a title insurance policy for both the lender and home buyer. These could be grouped into three categories: first-, second- and third-party claims.

First-party claims would be those initiated by a person who directly has or alleges to have an interest in the title. For instance, a recent divorcee, a forgotten heir or a relative who might be able to establish that the previous owner was in a diminished capacity and without the presence of mind to act reasonably, such as a parent suffering from Alzheimer's Disease, could pose a threat to the full or partial legitimacy of the deed.

Bad actors committing forgery, fraud, or presenting themselves as a false authority may create an issue with ownership rights. Shockingly, according to a study commissioned by the American Land Title Association [ALTA] and produced by Milliman, Inc., title insurance policy claims relating to fraud and forgery have more than doubled in recent years, rising to 44% of this group of first-party claims, versus 27% in the previous year of 2021 and an average of less than 20% in the prior part of the decade. They largely point to cybercrime as the vehicle for the increase in this type of malfeasance. The report also asserts that the cost to insurers for this rising number of fraud and forgery incidents averages more than $143,000 per claim. (Milliman, Inc., 2024)

Second-parties who had a tangential right to the proceeds of the sale of the property could also arise that would be protected by a title insurance policy. This could be a legitimate lien that was simply not recorded or went unrecorded in error, escaped the title check, or was granted in the narrow window between the title check but prior to the transaction. Or it could be a tax lien or special assessment levied by a condo or homeowners association but unpaid prior to the conveyance of title. Any type of lien or judgment that was not satisfied at the time of sale would still be attached to the property after the transaction and the new deed was recorded. And in case of such an oversight, rather than the new owner assume the debt, the lender or owner's title insurance policy would cover the pre-existing lien. This illustrates a distinct difference in title insurance in that it pertains to matters of fact prior to the change in title as opposed to other types of insurance that are liable for incidents that take place after an initial policy date.

Third-party vendors may create another source of contention where a title insurance policy may provide coverage from monetary loss. These could arise from procedural or clerical errors and/or omissions by the lender, surveyor, home inspector, realtor, notary, loan originator, even the title company itself or any third party involved in a purchase or refinance transaction.

Another concern that the ALTA report sheds light on to justify the expense of title insurance is that it may take years for these issues to surface. Nearly one third of claims are recognized within the first two years. Yet the final third of claims are reported after the fifth year and over the course of the next ten years. The total cost to cure defects in title amounts to approximately $500 million per year on average according to their data.

In the course of providing an insurance policy, a title company will provide a Title Commitment Letter for review by the lender but that also may be reviewed by the seller and buyer. This letter outlines any known liens, judgements, and/or attachments to the property that must be satisfied prior to policy issuance. The Closing Protection Letter is also furnished to the lender which specifically relieves the lender from mistakes that might be made by the title company or its agents.

A title company also provides and charges fees for other services necessary to complete a purchase or refinance transaction. In the normal course of business, they will obtain a "tax certificate" from the county or counties to confirm the seller pays their portion due up until the transaction settlement date. This information is also used to determine that a sufficient amount of money is funded into an escrow account when one is required or opted to be utilized and the correct monthly amount is billed for future impounds so adequate funds are available when the taxes are due.

Along with the escrow reserve funds and monthly impounds, the title company will work with the lender to each verify and cross-check that the proper amounts have been calculated correctly for all accounting matters related to the transaction. In effect, all monies for the transaction are collected and disbursed by the title company and their escrow agent. This includes but may not be limited to the earnest money deposit for a purchase, any and all invoices for third party vendors to the transaction, any debts that are to be satisfied, and the payment of any further proceeds of the transaction such as cash paid to the seller or cash paid to the owner subsequent to a refinance.

Customarily, the title company also provides the notary services required for owners, buyers and sellers to sign the documents related to each transaction. And most commonly, the final transaction documents will be signed at the title company office.

11. Survey

A residential land title survey is a map, named a plat, that numerically defines a location, called metes, and the extent of that parcel, known as bounds. The map illustrates the exact location and boundaries of the property along with where the house, improvements, and certain other features may lie within those land boundaries.

Noting the example in Exhibit 11-1, the legal description of the property is stated at the top of the survey. The survey is corroborated by the title company with a review matching its legal description to that of the title and deed.

The map will state a bearing and distance to at least one landmark of a recognizable and immovable object, such as the distance to a street corner. From that specific point, it will provide lines of latitude and longitude that form a geometric container.

Within that boundary, the diagram also provides measurements of the foundation, sidewalks and driveways drawn to scale. Additionally, it would include in the sketch any other improvements such as a patio, shed, barn, or pool.

Other elements that are part of a survey when applicable are visible natural elements like creeks, streams, ponds and water wells. Non-visible items may also be included, such as a buried septic tank, flood zones, and/or easements.

Easements can be thought of as an allowable access to a certain part of the property or a pathway. For example, in the rear of contiguous backyards, an easement may allow a septic tank pumping truck or heating oil delivery truck to cross the land and access the neighbor's property. Thus, the inclusion of easements is especially important as a survey is helpful to avoid future disputes. To this end, and for an additional fee, a survey can be staked, usually with inch thick, foot long steel pegs with a yellow cap to provide the identifiable four corners of the property, or more, when necessary.

These can be left in the ground and may prove useful as a reference for landscaping, plantings, lawn mowing or if fencing is desired in the future.

A professional survey might be expected to cost more than an appraisal, toward a $1,000 or more depending upon the size of the property. With new construction or if there have been any added improvements, a survey may be required the lender when financed. This may be paid for by the seller, typically, or the buyer on negotiated terms. However, some states allow for previous land surveys to be used with purchase transactions on existing properties. Therefore, it is highly advantageous to keep the survey and an additional copy in two separate and secure locations for good measure.

Exhibit 11-1

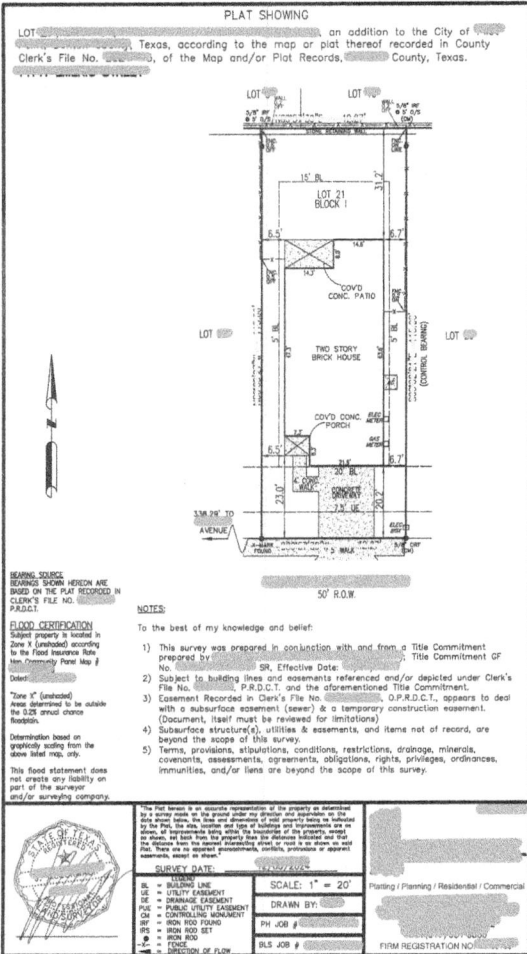

Make Your Mortgage Matter

12.   Moving

Moving can become very expensive. Perhaps as a young adult with few belongings this is a minimal expense if nothing more than a tank of gas, some pizza and a cold case with the help of a few friends. But later in life, with a family of four or more with several rooms of furniture, refrigerators, a freezer, a kitchen of cookware, a washer and dryer, an attic of seasonal decorations and a garage of tools and lawn equipment, moving becomes one of the most arduous tasks in life. Beyond physical labor and cost there is the emotional toll. It has been said that moving ranks as one of the top three most stressful life events along with changing jobs and getting married.

To ease that stress, hiring a moving company comes at no small expense. There are always many movers to choose from at varying costs based on the level of service, the number of possessions, and the distance between locations. A local move for a family of three from an apartment to a house may cost only about $1,500 just to move the boxes and furniture. Moving locally from house to house, again just the boxes and furniture, and the total bill might start to approach $5,000. And, so it is worthy of a line item in the budget.

Although people seem to buy a house with the intention of staying put for decades, the reality is that most people tend to move on average about every six years. If that turns out to be six times throughout the course of an adult life, those moving expenses can really add up.

PART 2: MORTGAGE FAVORABILITY

"From a money making point of view the only criterion for playing is whether you're a favorite in the game or an underdog. If you're a significant favorite, then it's a good game, and you should stay in it; if you're an underdog, then it's a bad game which you should quit."

-David Sklansky
The Theory of Poker

13.   The Definition of Mortgage

A mortgage is a loan to a borrower, the mortgagor, provided by a lender, the mortgagee. What specifically makes a mortgage different than other loans is that it involves real estate as collateral. A mortgage has two parts. First, the borrower gets a loan of money with an obligation to repay but also the right to repay any amount or all of the remaining balance of that loan at any time. The second part of the mortgage is the borrower's pledge of real estate, where the borrower grants the lender the right to seize and sell the property if the borrower fails to repay the loan as promised. (Fabozzi, The Handbook of Mortgage-Backed Securities, 2001, 1995)

There are really three contractual agreements that work in conjunction with each other. First, the mortgage, the agreement to offer real estate collateral in exchange for a loan. Second, the promissory note defining the specific loan amount, interest rate, and repayment terms. Third, the deed of trust, which allows the lender to place a title lien on the real estate property, prioritizing their right to recoup the balance of the loan amount and any expenses involved in doing so if the borrower defaults on the promissory note.

It is not at all the intention nor the desire of a lender to foreclose on the property, the process of seizing and selling as granted by the deed of trust. The lender is really a middle man who almost always sells the mortgage to an investor. The investor truly only ever wants the return of their money along with the promised interest rate of the loan.

The business of a foreclosure is the job of the loan servicer, to whom the mortgage payment is made by the borrower. The servicer is the bill collector and when the payments cease to be made, they are responsible for getting as much of the investor's money back as possible. But they do not guarantee any amount.

In the event of a foreclosure, the servicing company first recoups the costs accumulated throughout the liquidation process. Servicing companies incur numerous large expenses as they are generally mandated through their contractual agreement with the promissory note holder to do many things to limit capital losses. These may include but are not limited to considerable outreach to the borrower in an attempt to cure any delinquent payments (when 30 days past due), seeking to mitigate losses when a default is triggered (generally when a payment is more than 90 days late) by offering the borrower a reasonable plan to avoid foreclosure with a loan modification or other remedy, legal costs to foreclose when necessary, paying the property taxes and homeowners insurance when due, property maintenance, and advancing unpaid but scheduled principal and interest payments to the note holder. Next, the senior lien holder (typically the first mortgage lender) gets back the remaining principal balance of their loan, then any junior lien holders in order of when they placed their liens, and the remainder of money left over, if any, goes to the borrower. This is true at the time of any sale whether it is forced or not.

As an example, let's say a home was purchased for $500,000 with a down payment of $100,000 and a mortgage of $400,000. After a few years the value goes up to $550,000 and the balance is paid down to $390,000. But then, unfortunately, the borrower loses their job and becomes delinquent on the promissory note payments. As a result, and despite all efforts to avoid the inevitable, a foreclosure ensues forcing out the borrower and the loan servicing company hastily sells the property for $525,000 less 6% to the realtors, $493,500. The servicing company billed $25,000 for its default avoidance measures and also had to pay $25,000 to lawyers for the legal process, along with what was due over that time frame which included the mortgage interest that accrued, call it $12,000, $5,000 to the county for property taxes, $2,000 to the homeowners insurance company, and $1,000 to the HOA. Secondly, the first-lien holder gets their $390,000. Next, if they existed, would be any junior lien holder. In this scenario, despite the default and foreclosure, the borrower would still be entitled to the balance of the liquidation proceeds, receiving a check for $33,500.

However, let's say the economy tanked and not only did the borrower lose their job but a lot of other people did, too. In this scenario, the house might only sell for $450,000 less the realtor's 6%, $423,000. The servicing company still gets fully reimbursed for their outlays of $70,000. The investor is left with only $353,000 of the $390,000 loan balance they are owed. Despite a 20% down payment and only a 10% drop in home price value, the lender loses money and the borrower receives zero.

The burden of capital loss, money lent but not returned, is the risk and responsibility of the investor. Therefore, it is the investor that determines the parameters of the mortgages that they will purchase from any lender. This is the main focus of Part 2.

There are two broad mortgage categories, commercial and residential, and many subcategories of each. Residential real estate is defined as any property with only 4 dwelling units or less. A loan for any other real estate will typically be defined as a commercial mortgage. In this regard, a "land loan" provided to purchase or refinance raw land with no improvement is a commercial loan. A construction loan would follow, which is a mortgage on raw land with consideration for the near future value of a planned improvement, a house. This type of loan is short term financing that almost always is dependent on a commitment by the borrower to refinance into a residential mortgage.

Somewhat similar is a renovation loan, often referred to as a "fix and flip." This is, however, a residential mortgage based on the near future value of a current house with specified restorations, improvements of an improvement, to be completed along a well-defined timeline. At the other end of the spectrum, one might consider a reverse mortgage where the borrower draws out the capital value of the house but without the obligation of repayment, rather, in exchange for diminishing equity. These are both good examples of the usefulness and variety of specialized residential mortgages.

Most residential mortgages fall into two categories, a purchase or refinance. Purchase money mortgages are provided based on the current value of a property according to the lesser of an agreed upon purchase price or the appraised value. These can be refinanced based on the current appraised value for the sake of obtaining a more favorable rate and/or payment, or to access equity, a "cash-out refinance," to be used for any purpose. The most common use is for debt consolidation as the interest rate and payment is often substantially lower than the interest rate of credit card debt. Both of these types of loans are offered as a first lien mortgage where the lender requires being in a senior position to any other financing on the property.

A subordinate lien mortgage would be a home improvement loan, pool loan, or a second-lien mortgage. These are usually in the form of a closed-end loan where there is a set amount borrowed in one lump sum, or a revolving loan called a home equity line of credit [HELOC]. Again, the use of this money can be for debt consolidation or most any other purpose.

The lien position, senior or 1st versus junior or subordinate or 2nd, recognizes who gets their money back in the event of a refinance or transfer of title such as a sale or foreclosure. Being first, second, third and so on is ranked by the chronological order based on when the lien was recorded against the title. Accordingly, any second-lien loans will have a slightly higher prevailing interest as the risk for a loss is greater than a first-lien mortgage which has a priority position in the distribution of funds from the liquidation of the property.

Federal IRS tax liens, state income tax liens, and municipal property tax liens are instances which will supersede the right of even the first lien holder to recoup their capital first. Tax liens jump the line.

Judgements from any court orders will usually receive their money after all lien holders have been satisfied. Certain other creditors with ties to the real estate, like past due property association fees, will have their claims paid prior to the title holder. This is all in effect to provide a clean title to the next property buyer.

Make Your Mortgage Matter

14. Eligibility

A mortgage, promissory note and deed of trust are binding legal contracts. In order to be valid, the borrower must be 18 years of age and considered to have the capacity to enter into the agreement. Like any other legal contract, a signatory must have the mental capacity to understand the agreement. Of course, they must also be signing by their own free will, not under undue stress or demand by another party. The final signing of mortgage documents is witnessed by a notary who is typically specializes in mortgage closings.

With regard to the borrower, lenders are particularly concerned about two things, a borrower's history demonstrating an ability to manage debt payment obligations and their future ability to afford the additional new debt.

Of utmost relevance to a mortgage lender with regard to the borrower's credit history is their management of previous mortgage debt, if any. Found in Section 5: Declarations of the Uniform Residential Loan Application (URLA, see Appendix B) are direct questions of this nature. Any previous history of a default, foreclosure or bankruptcy will require several years of time elapsed before being eligible for a mortgage again. This clock begins when the final proceedings transpire, such as the court dismissal date from a Chapter 7 bankruptcy. These documents are important to retain as they will be necessary to provide to any future lender.

Just as detrimental to the possibility of future financing are late payments on any mortgage debt. This is not dependent on the property being financed, as even late payments on a timeshare will carry just as much of a seasoning requirement. Nearly without exception what appears on the borrower's credit report will be the only evidence a lender will consider, despite whatever story, mishap, or banking error was made by the borrower or by the creditor reporting the late payments and regardless of any documentation to the contrary. Late payments on any and all residential real estate debt will normally require some passing of time before a borrower may again be eligible for a real estate finance transaction.

The number and frequency of delinquent mortgage payments will vary from loan program to lender. Just one single payment marked as 30 days late within the most recent 12-month period may disqualify a borrower from specific loan programs that offer the best rates, or from a streamline refinance transaction, as examples. One payment shown as 90 days late may require 24 months to elapse prior to regaining eligibility. The repercussions from being late on a mortgage payment by 30 days or more can be severe. Because it is mortgage-related debt it is looked at closely when evaluating whether or not to lend to a potential borrower.

A credit report will also show late payments on other non-real estate debt obligations. However, those are not inspected as closely. The negative impact they have on a consumer's credit score is enough consideration for a mortgage lender. However, those accounts cannot show as late at the time of the credit report nor may any account be over the approved credit limit.

Establishing credit matters, too, along with demonstrating an ability to make timely payments on those lines of credit. Typically, most loan programs will require at least two accounts that have been open for twenty-four months or three accounts that have been open for twelve months (2x24 or 3x12).

This is not to say that a balance must be carried on these lines of credit. A healthy aversion to debt or owing anybody money is praiseworthy. It is the proof of being a trustworthy debtor that is sought. And in some circumstances, it is the access to debt that can be critical, maybe to avoid being short on cash for a mortgage payment due in the future.

There are three nationally recognized credit bureaus and a score must be provided by all three in order to meet most mortgage eligibility standards. With regard to what that score must be is a moving target. But for the sake of brevity, a goal of 680 or higher is pretty good standard. A more thorough discussion on the impact of a credit score is provided within the upcoming chapter on Loan Level Price Adjustments.

The second fundamental criteria to lending is an assessment of the borrower's ability to meet the proposed monthly mortgage payment obligation. There are at least two ways that a borrow may do so, the most common of which is based on their monthly income.

The second way is based on their ability to liquidate assets. To keep it simple, if a borrower has ten million dollars in a brokerage account invested in the stock market or other highly liquid, accessible, and fungible asset (as of January 1, 2024, this would not include cryptocurrencies), then it is proper to assume they can sell a portion each month to meet their cash needs and fulfill any debt obligations. Two to six months of statements showing that $10,000,000 balance would suffice.

An income calculation can be more complicated. And so too is the degree to which that income is viewed as reliable. Two years of employment history within the same industry is the standard. But, to start from the beginning, a recent high school or college graduate may only be required to show one pay stub along with an offer letter stating their expected annual wages. School counts as a substitute for those two years of employment.

A person changing employers within the same industry may also only need to show one pay stub from the new employer along with an offer letter. A person not transitioning into a job at a new employer can be expected to provide one month of pay stubs, so two pay stubs if paid bi-monthly or 24 times per year. Alternatively, this might be three pay stubs if paid bi-weekly or 26 times per year. And, of course, just one if paid monthly.

Depending on their length of employment, the gross earnings before any deductions from those pay stubs must pencil out to the average amount paid year to date. As an example, an hourly employee who generally only work 25 hours per week cannot work

40 hours per week for the month of August just to be able to use those pays stubs for a juiced-up income calculation. On the other hand, someone who receives a documented raise would be the beneficiary of an income calculation based on the new pay rate despite their year-to-date income being lower than what would be expected from the most recent month's income.

The requirements are slightly different when more than 50% of an employee's income is generated from commission. Their year-to-date commission income will only be admissible if they have maintained a similar portion of income for the previous two years within the same industry.

Employees will also be required to provide the previous year or two's W2s from any and all employers over that time frame. A W2 is required by law to be provided to each employee at the beginning of the year. It shows the total gross earnings and deductions from the prior year.

Overtime and bonuses may also be used if supported by previous W2s and confirmed by a Verification of Employment. This document is usually supplied by the lender directly to the employer in the later stages of the loan application and approval process. Among other things, it asks for the previous year's overtime and bonuses and whether or not they reasonably expect that additional pay to continue. Knowing that an annual bonus or overtime is part of an agreed upon compensation structure, then it may be okay to use as part of an initial income calculation.

Self-employed business owners need rely upon their IRS tax returns to identify the income needed to calculate their ability to meet all their debt obligations including the new mortgage payment. The adjusted gross income from the previous two years of tax returns is required to be used for most loan programs. Alternatively, some loan programs allow the most recent 12 or 24 months of bank statements where only regular and usual deposits are calculated against an industry specific or standard expense ratio as a source to calculate average monthly income.

The amount identified from the most recent year must be an increase from the previous year in order to use the average of both years. If the most recent year's income is less, then that lesser most recent year's income is used. Along with the income, evidence of licensure that the business has existed for two years is often also required.

Much simpler to document is Social Security income. Early on each year the recipient receives a Benefit Statement stating the monthly benefit to be received. This is the letter that is used to confirm this income.

Pensions and scheduled 401(k) and/or IRA payments are other sources of income easily documented.

Disabled veterans may receive a VA Disability Benefit that may also be used as income to qualify for a mortgage payment.

Generally speaking, all of the above can be used on a mixed basis. Meaning, income from multiple sources as well as income from co-borrowers may be used to demonstrate an ability to repay debt obligations. However, adding a co-borrower's income requires consideration of their credit score and the total combined debt obligations, too.

Part of the work of a licensed mortgage loan originator is to determine the allowable income to be used to qualify for a mortgage payment. Their review of the credit report is to verify the borrower meets the standards as previously discussed. The report also provides the details of all other monthly debt obligation payments that will be factored against the allowable income in addition to the anticipated new mortgage payment. A loan originator also assesses the amount and source of funds of the down payment in part to comply with anti-money laundering regulations. The Uniform Residential Loan Application provides further insight into what all lenders consider when reviewing a borrower's eligibility for loan programs.

Finding and working with a very experienced loan originator is key to mortgage success. A thorough initial review, attention to detail and proper calculations will not guarantee that other deal breaking issues won't come up in the underwriting process. But a loan originator's mistakes or oversight committed early on will almost certainly be caught by the processor, underwriter, closer or any other set of eyes whom also review the all documentation prior to any final loan approval. This may ultimately lead to ineligibility or, although less disappointingly, switching to a more costly loan program than anticipated.

Maybe more importantly, one mortgage loan originator may have the insight to recommend a far superior loan program offered by their lender while another originator at the same lender might not realize that it would be more appropriate for that same borrower. Unfortunately, it would be nearly impossible for the borrower to know that a better option was available. They simply would not know what they don't know.

Finding a professional, very experienced loan originator can be problematic for borrowers. Relying on a lender's reputation does not ensure being paired with a knowledgeable originator. Indeed, licensing requirements and continuing education focus primarily on compliance with lending rules and regulations and pay very little, if any, attention to evaluating the financial implications between the many mortgage products available, let alone the choices that can be made in arranging the elements within any particular mortgage.

The tool that a borrower is provided to compare one possible mortgage versus another offered from a different lender is the Loan Estimate (see Appendix C). The Loan Estimate is standardized form that must be provided to a borrower within three days of completing a loan application with a lender. This estimate is the proposal for a mortgage that the loan originator believes they can provide to the borrower based on their initial review of only the application and credit report. The details found on the Loan Estimate are helpful in evaluating the mortgage.

Although time consuming, a borrower really ought to interview a loan originator from several different lenders and complete applications with at least three within the same day or two.

By doing so, a borrower will then have at least three mortgage options to compare. They will also have the opportunity to think about which loan originator they may want to work with over the next two to six weeks. Understand these are not mutually exclusive. Maybe one originator presents a deal with a loan that appears structurally better than the other two. It might be prudent to ask the other loan originators to provide new estimates with similar loan attributes. The intention is to compare green apples to green apples although an orange may still be better.

The interest rate is not the only item to compare. The Loan Estimate provides an APR that is often thought of as the most efficient way to compare similar loans. The number itself has no bearing but it is a simple way to combine the interest rate and the transaction costs for the loan. A better, back of the envelope calculation is to multiply the monthly principal and interest payment times the number of payments, add to that the "Estimated Cash to Close" and deduct items F, G, and H. On a purchase, this would be the total amount paid for the house if only the minimum payments were made as scheduled.

This calculation seeks to eliminate most items that can be used to manipulate a loan estimate that make it appear to be better or inadvertently worse than another loan estimate. Items F, G and H are property tax and homeowners insurance estimates. The lender is not held accountable for these to be accurate. Only items A, B, and C need to be within a tolerance of error. However, with any significant change in the loan parameters, a lender may change these costs. The costs shown on an original Loan Estimate may be different than the last Loan Estimate received.

The Closing Disclosure (Appendix D) reveals the difference between only the most recently provided Loan Estimate and the approximate or actual final costs. For borrowers financing a primary residence or second house, the Closing Disclosure is required to be provided three days in advance of the day the final mortgage documents will be signed. This allows the borrower time to review the documents for any errors.

On a purchase transaction, once the final documents are signed with a notary present, the deal is done and the loan will be funded. On a refinance, borrowers are allotted three days to review the final mortgage documents before the loan is consummated. During this time, if something is found to be amiss by either the borrower or the lender, either party has the opportunity to request a change or nullify the transaction. For instance, a lender may seek to verify that the borrower is still employed during this time and/or continue to monitor their credit for any significant changes. Or a borrower may just change their mind and decide they don't want to refinance. More subtly, there could be an error in a figure that could be detected during this three day right of rescission. The number could be corrected, the documents redrawn and the closing with the notary completed again.

15.   Loan Amount

"How much can I afford?" is the best question to ask when considering financing a home with a mortgage. The regulatory standard for qualifying mortgage borrowers is to determine the borrower's ability to repay. But that ability only needs to be considered for the next three years which is kind of silly when mortgages are paid back over thirty years. But who knows what the future holds. Someone who qualifies based on their current income today is not guaranteed to have a job tomorrow. In which case, they may not be able to afford their very first mortgage payment. So, truthfully, from an investor's point of view, the only practical reduction of risk is based on the amount of the loan versus the value of the collateral. This is known as loan-to-value [LTV]. The lower the loan-to-value, the less risk for the lender.

The same could be said for the borrower. Recall the hierarchy of liquidation proceeds. A borrower is more than likely to lose all of their equity or cash value with a minimal initial equity-to-value [ETV]. From a mental perspective, the more equity a borrower has in the property, the more likely they are to do everything possible to avoid a foreclosure and risk having that investment wiped out in a liquidation where they have no control over the negotiation of the sales price.

Contrarily, when a borrower has invested only a small sum of money into the purchase of a home, they are likely to be more apathetic with regard to losing that equity. They have little skin in the game, so to speak. Investors understand this psychology and therefore often require additional insurance against potential losses when lending more than 80% of the house value. Loans above 80% LTV are certainly available, but because of the additional mortgage insurance required, they decrease the affordability of the house.

An argument could be made that allowing borrowers to finance a higher percentage of a house's value has, over the years, only resulted in driving up house values. The idea that being able to borrow 85, 90, or 95% of the value of a house makes that house more affordable is entirely laughable. The monthly payment is higher.

In other words, consider two houses side by side of equal value but two different buyers. The first buyer provides a 20% down payment and the buyer of the second house invests only 5%. The second buyer's monthly mortgage payment could easily be 25 to 50% more. And when only scheduled payments are made, the second buyer could be encumbered by that additional mortgage insurance for three to twelve years. Even in a best-case scenario where home price appreciation allowed the second buyer to drop the mortgage insurance in three years, they are still financing more money from the outset. For a house purchased at the same price, the second buyer financing 95% could easily end up paying 50% or much more, hundreds of thousands of dollars for a median priced home.

Viewed in a different light, to have equal payments with only a 5% down payment versus a 20% stake equates to purchasing a house that is valued around 30% less. Consider this notion in terms of affordability if both buyers are earning the same. Expressed another way, someone who borrows $400,000 on a $500,000 house would have a payment nearly the same as someone who borrows $332,500 on a $350,000 house.

Down payment assistance programs do little to provide relief to this dilemma. Rather, they may encourage borrowers to enter a situation that may be ill advised. In absolute terms, paying total costs of 50% to 100% more for any item as a result of increased financing costs ought to dissuade a prudent person from entering into that transaction. But the deal is not presented nor exposed from that point of view.

However, these programs may indeed be the best-case scenario for a home purchase and do quite a bit of good. They reduce the initial barrier to entry for homeownership despite the increased acquisition costs over time. Initially or eventually the monthly house payment will almost certainly be less than the cost to rent.

Most down payment assistance programs are sponsored by state or municipal organizations. Eligibility varies with each program but is usually based on municipal employment or income. Firefighters, law enforcement, educators, medical staff and other groups of civil employees may find programs available to them. Alternatively, qualification for this type of down payment assistance might be based on income. The thresholds vary from program to program, but are likely require falling below the county's median income or otherwise being considered to have a low income in relation to others within that specific zip code. It may be worth a little extra research if you fall into either of these two categories.

These are certainly beneficial programs when used in conjunction with other funds to increase the down payment or increase the initial equity to value. Gift funds are another viable option. Most underwriting criteria allow gift funds of any amount as long as they are provided by a past, present or future family member.

Seller concessions, also known as interested party contributions, are a bargaining tool that can increase equity and should be utilized to do so in many situations. In addition to the purchase price, buyers must also pay for the transaction costs. As an example, perhaps a buyer chooses to buy a house that is listed for $300,000. In one scenario, the buyer offers 95% of the asking price which is accepted. The borrower is able to provide a down payment of $45,000 but also must pay all of the closing costs that amount to $15,000. They will be required to source $60,000 and borrow $240,000. With a loan to value of 84.2%, they will pay mortgage insurance.

In another scenario, the buyer offers 100% of the asking price with the stipulation of a 5% seller contribution. The two scenarios are a wash for the seller, they get almost the same proceeds either way. And the buyer in both scenarios borrows $240,000. But in the second scenario, the seller concession pays the closing costs so that the entirety of the buyer's funds goes toward equity. This borrower ends up financing only 80%, likely with a better interest rate and most definitely without the additional monthly cost of mortgage insurance.

Imagine that. In this second scenario, the borrower pays more for the house, brings the same amount of cash to the bargaining table, and walks away with a lower monthly payment.

It should be noted that VA loans are a different animal. Veterans may and probably should finance 100% of the purchase price and the closing costs, without any ongoing mortgage insurance, and yet typically with one of the lowest interest rates available in residential real estate finance. Still, the mortgage payment and all housing expenses need to be affordable. But any other consideration for providing an additional but unnecessary down payment ought to be compared as an opportunity cost of where else that money might be invested or the benefit of increasing the nest egg.

16. Payment-to-Income Ratio

When asked by a borrower how much one can afford, unfortunately, the default response from most lenders and mortgage loan originators is based on how large of a mortgage they can provide based on a singular approach to measure the ability to repay, the debt-to-income ratio [DTI]. Borrowers ought to consider multiple metrics as a prudent way to know what is safely affordable.

Probably the oldest form of guidance regarding how much should be spent on housing expense is the payment-to-income ratio, or PTI. This amounts to a pretty simple budget item, really. This is no different than considering current monthly rent as a percentage of income. Technically speaking, the calculation is the total of the new monthly mortgage principal and interest payment, property taxes and hazard or homeowners insurance whether it is included as a payment to an escrow account or not, flood insurance if required, and property owners' association dues, if any, divided by the total amount of verified monthly gross income.

The PTI is also known as the front-end ratio where the back-end ratio (or debt-to-income ratio [DTI]) includes other monthly obligations, like an auto loan or lease payment, divided by monthly gross income. The government subscribed maximum expenditure for total obligations is 50% of income. This is true even when a borrower has no monthly debt servicing payments other than the proposed housing payment, where the PTI and DTI are the same. In this scenario, a full 50% of gross income would be allocated to their cost of housing.

Historically, only 20% of an individual or family's income was thought of as a normal guideline for how much should be budgeted toward their housing expense. (U.S. Department of Housing and Urban Development Office of Policy Development and Research, 2017) Gradually, that 20% has drifted upward to 50% which does not confer affordability but really the opposite (see Chapter 1).

One extremely important clarification is the divisor in both ratios is the gross income or income before any deductions from a paycheck. (Selling Guide, 2024) Realize this isn't 50% of take-home pay, but, for the median income borrower, it is now more like 60 to 70% of net pay.

It would be far more conservative to apply this rule of thumb for housing payment affordability based on a borrower's net pay after deductions. The dramatic increase in cost of health insurance premiums is enough of a reason to take this approach. According to a report by KFF, the average annual premium for family coverage in 1999 was $5,791. By 2022, that premium had soared to $22,463. (2023 Employer Health Benefits Survey, 2023) What this means is that American families have far less disposable income than had previously been available to pay their housing expense. But there has been no adjustment in the analysis of a borrower's ability to afford their housing payment. There is no accounting for health insurance premiums, deductibles or other expenses in the mortgage approval process. This is an industry oversight, but the individual should be aware of this and make certain it is accounted for in their budget.

Another potential oversight is that PTI and DTI do not include utilities, like water, gas, electric, garbage collection, sewer fees or internet access. All these necessities add up to a big bill depending on the municipality and are clearly housing related expenses. (Consumer Expenditures and Income: Overview, 2022) Regardless of location, homes are required to have a permanent heat source in order to be financed. But there is no consideration for the cost of that heat.

When considering housing affordability, it is important to draw a distinction between how much you may want to spend versus how much the lender says you can spend.

17.   Debt-to-Income Ratio

The debt-to-income ratio, or DTI, is the most common calculation used to measure a borrower's ability to repay. Technically, the ratio is the total of the new monthly mortgage principal and interest payment, property taxes and hazard or homeowners insurance whether it is included as a payment to an escrow account or not, flood insurance if required, property owners' association dues, plus those same existing payments on any other real estate or land owned, plus all monthly debt servicing payments shown on the credit report divided by the total amount of verified monthly gross income. In most cases this is the sum of all the required payments on real estate, auto, credit card, student loans and any other installment debt, divided by the monthly gross income prior to any deductions.

Factually it is known that below a 30% DTI, mortgage defaults are rare, but above 30%, defaults increase proportionally. (Fram, Gerardi, Sexton, & Tracy, 2020) For manually underwritten loans that can be sold to FNMA, the threshold is still a 36% DTI. In 2014, the Consumer Financial Protection Bureau [CFPB] implemented a rule that the maximum DTI could not exceed 43% unless a government sponsored enterprise was involved. But now, the regular DTI limit is 50% and even that can be pushed slightly higher in certain situations.

In reality, there is a terrible flaw with having a maximum DTI, specifically on a cash-out loan used for debt consolidation. One example is a borrower who over many years has amassed credit card and other debts so that along with their existing mortgage payment the current DTI would now be approaching 75%. That alone is a cautionary tale. Whereby using their home equity to pay off that debt, their new DTI would be around 55%, lower by nearly 20%. Imagine, too, they were never once late to pay their existing mortgage. By providing them a more affordable situation the likelihood of default on a new mortgage would make common sense. But because the DTI is over 50%, they would not be helped.

A borrower ought to inquire what the lender's computed DTI is because it is not disclosed on any of the loan documentation provided to them. It is also important to understand that even though a lender may be able to provide a mortgage with a DTI anywhere near, at or above 50%, that does not mean it is affordable. Much caution is prescribed in proceeding with a DTI above 40% unless there are other significant factors that reduce the risk of default. The national average DTI is just below 40%. Obviously, the lower DTI, the more affordable the payment.

18. Debt Service Coverage Ratio

The Debt Service Coverage Ratio or DSCR is a long-standing metric in the commercial real estate space that over the last decade has been applied by some residential real estate lenders. This is simply the rent payment divided by the mortgage payment. Technically, it is the rent payment divided by the total of the monthly mortgage principal and interest payment, property taxes and hazard or homeowners insurance whether it is included as a payment to an escrow account or not, flood insurance if required, and property owners' association dues, if any.

For a residential investment property purchase, the rent amount will be obtained from the comparable rent schedule, a supplement to the regular appraisal, or from an actual lease agreement. For the purposes of a refinance, if the property has been owned for more than two years, then the rent amount will be obtained from Schedule E of the borrower's federal tax returns.

Basically, if the rent is more than the payment, then the ratio is greater than 1.0 and the property is typically considered cash flow positive. However, it still may not be cash flow positive. What is not evaluated by this ratio is any loss of rental income when the property might be in between renters, referred to in annual terms as the vacancy rate. Nor does it take into account any maintenance, repairs, insurance deductibles, or any potential increases in property taxes, insurance or property owner's association dues.

The DSCR ratio can certainly be a useful tool for non-investors, too. At the very least, the ratio can be used to evaluate whether or not the purchase price is reasonable. Similar homes for rent in the neighborhood can provide an indication of rent. But even better, the DSCR can help solve the biggest flaw and mitigate some of the risk when relying solely on the debt-to-income ratio when determining an ability to repay.

Consider a borrower who loses their job, whether that is the day after they close on a purchase or years later. Before or without exhausting all of their savings or reserve funds, they may be much better off renting their home rather than being forced to sell and certainly rather than defaulting on their mortgage. If prior to purchase the DSCR is considered and the property is cash flow positive, then the borrower may have another option available to avoid foreclosure.

Note, however, that the comparable rent schedule will not be ordered as part of the appraisal for the purchase of a primary or secondary home. But it is possible to utilize other resources to obtain an indication of the rental value of the property.

19.   Savings and Reserves

When considering the affordability of a mortgage to purchase or refinance a home, a borrow would be wise to consider their ability to fund savings and reserve accounts. Surprisingly, this plays no written role in lending standards, guidelines, or in the discussions regarding housing affordability on FHA, VA, USDA, FNMA or FHLMC government sponsored loans.

Indeed, providing a mortgage at or near a 100% loan-to-value, LTV, and/or with a debt-to-income ratio, DTI, near 50% of gross income runs counter to encouraging savings. It also greatly increases the risk of default.

In order to purchase a home, it would be financially foolish to finance a home that requires a payment so large relative to one's current income that no money remains to fund or continue to grow any meaningful savings. What ought to also be considered extremely risky would be to provide a down payment that depletes all of one's savings and/or reserves.

Consider a person who spends every last dime to come up with the down payment and closing costs to buy a home. Believe it or not, this happens all the time. That family moves into the home and has zero money in the bank until their next paycheck arrives. Of a thousand unlucky circumstances, imagine what will happen if their car breaks down.

It could be argued that the first lesson in home economics would be to have a savings account. Wealth is best understood as having enough money available for future spending when required. This is the foundation of asset/liability management. Understanding when in the future cash will be required in order to meet expenses, along with excess cash available at all times for unplanned expenses are the hallmark of financial stability. Without either, debt is sure to grow.

It should be encouraged for all homebuyers to have a thorough budget with a line item for savings. This should also include all housing-related expenses in addition to the required mortgage payment. This will be discussed in greater detail in Part 3.

20. Interest Rate Determination

Mortgage interest rates vary depending on the perceived risks of each loan. This is known as risk-based pricing. From a lender or investor perspective, the first concern is to get back the entire loan amount or principal investment. Secondly, they want to make at least the same amount as if they had invested that money elsewhere. Third, they want to make some additional money to cover losses they may incur on other loans. And, last, they need to cover the business costs associated with loan origination and servicing obviously with the intention of making a profit.

So, when assessing the potential risk or reward of each individual loan, several risk factors are considered that may ultimately provide a rate that is higher or lower than the prevailing rate seen or heard quoted by general media sources, acquaintances, colleagues, neighbors, friends or family. In addition to the current interest rate on 10 Year US Treasurys, the factors that influence each mortgage's interest rate can be broken down into seven categories.

1. payment schedule
    a. maturity
    b. amortization
    c. interest
2. secondary market and mortgage insurance
3. loan level price adjustments
    a. purpose
    b. loan-to-value
    c. credit score
    d. property
4. prepayment penalty period
5. lender or borrower paid commission
6. discount, par, or premium pricing
7. rate lock period and extensions

Conceptually, each of these elements provide an up or down adjustment to the rate in a layered fashion. In other words, they are considered in combination with each other and some may have more, less or no bearing on the rate depending on the value of one or more of the other components. That is to say, it's complicated.

21.   Payment Schedule

The structure of a mortgage primarily consists of three elements, the maturity, amortization and interest rate which are all necessary to define a schedule of payments. These three items can be quite simple or often needlessly complex.

a. Maturity is meant to be when the final payment is due.
b. Amortization refers to the timing of scheduled repayments of principal.
c. Interest rate determines the monthly charge for the outstanding balance.

Maturity, amortization and interest variances are very co-dependent and any strategy to get the most out of a mortgage will consider them to be in alignment with the other six elements that function together to calculate the interest rate.

The most common term in the US is a 30-year, level pay, fixed rate mortgage. The payment schedule for this loan requires 360 equal monthly payments where the interest rate remains the same. Indeed, for most situations, this type of plain vanilla mortgage is wholly appropriate.

Keep in mind that with mortgages, the borrower, or mortgagor, always has the right to repay any or all of the loan amount at any time they desire. It's worth repeating, a partial repayment of principal in any amount can be made at any time and this is called a curtailment. This right of full or additional principal repayment is keenly important to building proper mortgage strategies.

a. Maturity

Most lenders will advertise 10, 15, 20, 25 and 30-year terms but they may also be able to offer mortgages with maturities ranging in any monthly increment from 120 to 360 months.

Terms shorter than ten years will likely be provided with a balloon feature. 7-year balloons used to be quite common. This would require the remaining principal balance be repaid entirely at that date although the monthly required payments for the first seven years would be the same as a 30-year mortgage.

When considering a shorter or longer term, the most important idea to be aware of is the incentive for being required to repay that loan sooner. As mentioned before, mortgage rates are built on risk-based pricing. And the longer money is lent, the more risk that conditions may deteriorate and limit the borrower's ability to repay. So, an investor receiving a shorter term should imply a loan with a lower interest rate provided as an incentive to the borrower for paying the money back sooner.

But this isn't always the case. The difference between a 15 and 30-year rate can be quite volatile and range anywhere from less than a quarter point when the yield curve is flat or inverted and as much as 1.00%. And also know that mortgages with terms of 120 to 180 months, or up to 15 years, are going to have similar rates. But anything longer, even just a 21-year term is going to have a rate much closer to a 30-year mortgage due to how they are pooled together in Mortgage-Backed Securities.

But even though a considerably lower rate may be available, other things ought to be considered that may be way more important. Although the rate may be lower, the payment on an amortizing loan will be higher so is the payment affordability is a huge consideration. Some people make the mistake of having a 15-year mortgage payment in a valiant effort to pay off their home but at the consequence of running up credit card debts at triple the interest rate.

The same payment affordability consideration should be levied based on a retirement horizon. In an ideal world, one might want to match the maturity with their retirement horizon. By this logic, they will not have a mortgage payment eating up their monthly retirement income. Even when that is the plan, if refinancing a mortgage for a lower rate, which is a great thing, one still may want a 30-year mortgage. They can maintain the discipline of continuing to make the same payment they are used to making, or make a payment that will have the balance paid off at that retirement age goal. The required payment must be made, but any additional amount may be paid regularly or at any time.

On the contrary, if a mortgage won't be paid off entirely by retirement, refinancing to a new 30-year term prior to retirement may prove highly beneficial. This will allow a borrower to obtain a fixed payment as small as possible throughout retirement to allow stretching the retirement income as far as possible. In other words one ought to consider what matters more: having extra money in one 70s while still able to enjoy it; or, having a mortgage paid off when 79. And a word of caution, it is important to get this straight with working age regular income prior to retiring because a reduced retirement income may prevent one from refinancing despite a lower rate and/or payment. This has been the disappointing situation for many retirees.

b. Amortization

The word "mortgage" comes from the legal or judicial context of two Latin root words. "Mortuō" means decaying or withering away from, in this case, "wadium," later 'wadi' then which is to say a contract or pledge. In most mortgages, each payment pays a portion of the principal balance so that the balance gradually declines. With the last payment the balance of the loan is zero. Having fulfilled the obligation, the contract is no longer legally valid.

There are exceptions to this, of course, namely an Interest Only [IO] loan where no principal payment is required for an initial period of time or up until the final maturity date. Additionally, a balloon mortgage typically requires a portion of principal to be paid each month based on this decaying balance notion but a total payment in full is due much sooner, like an early death.

In addition to that principal amount the payment also consists of the monthly accrued interest. The accrued interest is $1/12^{th}$ of the annual interest rate times the outstanding principal balance at the beginning of the previous month. As an example, and to make the math easy, if the balance on January 1 is $100,000 and the interest rate is 12%, then on February 1st the accrued interest due for the month of January is 1% of $100,000 or $1,000. If the interest rate were only 6%, then the interest due would only be $500 (100,000 × .06 ÷ 12 = 500).

It's that simple to calculate the payment on a fixed rate, interest only mortgage and that would be the payment due each and every month. That is true until the loan would need to be repaid in full, whatever that maturity date may be, or an amortization period began.

If equal monthly principal payments were preferred, then $1/360^{th}$ of $100,000 is $277.78. Combined with the annual 6% rate, the interest due would be an additional $500 to total $777.78. With a balance of $99,500, the accrued interest due on the 1st day of the next month would be $497.50 and along with the $277.78, the total payment would be $775.28. Finally, on the 360th month, $500 in principal balance would be remaining and due along with $2.50 in interest, totaling $502.50. This would be a declining monthly required payment.

But again, the most common type of mortgage in the US is a 30-year level pay, fixed rate mortgage. What is a bit tricky to calculate is the amount of principal due that would also be required along with the interest so the balance is zero with last payment while the same payment is due each month.

(original balance×((rate÷12)×(1+rate÷12)^(term))÷((1+rate÷12)^(term)-1))

Using amortization with the above example, the equal payments would be $599.55. With the first payment, $500 would be accrued interest due and $99.55 would reduce the principal balance to $99,900.45. Then on March 1, the accrued interest due would be $499.50 or 6.00% ÷ 12 × $99,900.45. And $100.05 would be credited toward the principal balance reducing it to $99,800.40.

A level pay, fixed rate mortgage that is fully amortizing is preferable because the payment is lower initially by $175. And it remains lower for the first 129 months, nearly 11 years. Applying that net higher payment amount as a curtailment to a traditional level pay mortgage would result in this loan being paid off within 24 years and a savings of nearly $10,000 in interest.

Finally, it is important to understand what is called a recast. This is when the amortization is recalculated to produce a revised level payment. This happens in two instances. The first and most common is when the interest rate changes on an adjustable-rate mortgage [ARM]. Know that when the rate adjusts periodically, a new principal & interest payment is calculated based on the number of months remaining until maturity, the remaining outstanding principal balance, and the new rate.

Secondly, some lenders may allow a recast on a level pay, fixed rate mortgage. Certain thresholds are usually required to be provided a recast, such as a new curtailment of at least 10% of the outstanding principal balance at the time of the request, perhaps some time having elapsed from the date of the loan origination, and perhaps a nominal fee to do so. A new payment would then be calculated based on the reduced principal balance, the same rate and same number of months remaining until maturity.

This may allow a mortgagor to reduce their required payment without the cost of refinancing and without changing the interest rate if it happens to be below the current market rate. But this may not always be advisable. It certainly could be advantageous for someone approaching retirement and looking to minimize the monthly payment subject to an expected reduction of monthly income. But this scenario also assumes a sizable principal payment and higher prevailing interest rates. So, opportunity cost might be a consideration. Basically, could that money be invested elsewhere producing more income than the amount of savings created by the recast.

c. Interest Rate

The interest rate is the third variable required to calculate a mortgage payment. An interest rate on a loan will be either fixed or floating. In the US, most residential loans are fixed rate mortgages or FRMs. A fixed interest rate implies that the rate remains constant throughout the life of the loan. With a level pay amortization and a fixed rate, the mortgage payment will not change. This is usually preferable because it is easier to manage in a budget.

A floating or Adjustable-Rate Mortgage [ARM], as opposed to a fixed rate, means the interest rate may change from time to time.

(To stem any confusion, "floating" is also used in another context. Initially, a quote of an interest rate may be provided by a loan originator. A borrower may choose not to lock in the rate immediately but elect to do so at some point prior to closing. This is considered "floating the rate." That quoted rate may change daily or even numerous times within a day until it is agreed to be locked. "Floating the rate" and a "floating rate mortgage" are two entirely different things.)

With the change in the interest rate periodically, based on prevailing interest rates, the mortgage payment will also change. And when it does, the required monthly minimum payment will also change. And that is where it gets complicated because there are many different offerings of when, why, and how that interest rate will change. And to understand how, maybe, to take advantage of those different possibilities without unwarranted risk requires some very serious expertise.

An ARM has three variables. The first is when that rate may change, the reset date. The second is what causes it to change, the index. And the third are the limitations to the change, the caps and floors.

The initial interest rate on an ARM will be fixed for one year and then will reset annually. Hybrid ARMS are fixed for a longer initial period, 3, 5, 7 or 10 years commonly and then often reset annually. For instance, a Hybrid ARM that has a fixed interest rate for the first 3 years and then may reset annually thereafter would be described as a 3/1 ARM.

When evaluating if an ARM is advantageous or too risky, it is paramount to understand shape of the yield curve. ARMs may offer a lower initial rate but only when the shape of the yield curve is positively sloped. Consider that if short term rates are a lot lower than slightly longer term rates, a steeply sloped curve, then a simple ARM is riskier in that the interest rate is more likely to reset higher, obviously, sooner than a 3/1 hybrid ARM and certainly risker still than a fixed rate mortgage that will remain constant. Therefore, it is logical that the longer time period that the initial rate is fixed, the more closely that initial rate will be to a 30-year fixed rate.

The change in rate is tied to an index plus the margin. The index has traditionally been the weekly average yield of actively traded US Treasury bills, notes, and bonds with a constant maturity of one year, or 1YR CMT as published by the Federal Reserve. There are other common indexes such as COFI or a Cost of Funds Index of which there are two, one published by the Federal Home Loan Bank of San Francisco and another by the Office of Thrift Supervision. 6-month LIBOR [London Interbank Offered Rate] used to be very common but has been replaced with the Secured Overnight Financing Rate [SOFR]. (Kagan, 2024) The real takeaway here is that the index is going to be pre-determined and a reflection of lending rates for the time period until the next reset.

On top of the index is the margin. The margin can be understood as the compensation the lender receives for the credit risk of the borrower. From a lender's perspective, if one can invest money in US Treasurys every year over and over again without taking any perceivable risk whatsoever, then in order to lend or invest it elsewhere that same investor would expect to be rewarded in a measure equal to the excess risk. And that difference is the margin a mortgagor will need to pay the investor.

Both the investor or mortgagee and the mortgagor are protected to some extent from dramatic shifts in interest rates in a floating rate mortgage. The initial cap and floor are the maximum that the rate may change in relation to the original interest rate at the first reset date. The periodic cap and floor are the maximum the rate may change in relation to the current rate at any subsequent reset date after the initial reset date. The lifetime cap is the maximum increase from the original interest rate.

The index plus the margin will be the rate at the reset date but limited by the caps and floors. Let's consider an example of a 5.00% 5/1 1/2/3 at 1YRCMT +250. The original interest rate will be 5.00% for five years and then reset annually, that is the "5/1" part. The next set of numbers, the "1/2/3" define the initial cap, the periodic cap from the second adjustment date and beyond, and finally, the maximum change in percentage points from the original interest rate. Therefore, at the first reset date, the most the rate could increase would be 1.00% to 6.00% if the index were at or above 3.500%. At the seven-year mark, the rate could increase at most by 2.00% to 8.00%, if the index were at or above 5.500%. And the rate could not increase beyond that as the aggregate increase is limited to 3.00%. This works in either direction, too. The rate would not decrease by more than 1% in year 6. And the lowest the rate could be in year 7 is 5-1-2=2.000% but the index would need to be -0.50% or less for that to happen.

The initial rate offered on an ARM or Hybrid ARM is often considered a teaser rate. It is called so because it lures a borrower into accepting the risk of a future higher rate. When rates are historically low, there may be little short-term benefit in a slightly lower initial rate versus the fixed rate offering, likely not enough to justify the exposure of the rate adjusting higher periodically. In that low interest rate environment where the Ten Year Treasury is closer to zero, probability would favor rates going higher (see Chapter 32.) A floating rate may only be preferable, generally speaking, when rates seem historically high and there exists a greater likelihood that rates may fall or at least stay close to the same. The teaser rate in this situation may be relatively lower than the fixed rate offering.

Realize however, that with a fixed rate mortgage, the borrower is always protected from rising interest rates. And they are also unencumbered to refinance except by transaction costs, credit worthiness, and income qualification. Mortgage borrowers retain the right to refinance their mortgage at any time and tend to do so when dramatic decreases in interest rates present a significant savings to do so. A fixed rate mortgage will also favor the borrower when interest rates are well above recent averages.

22. Secondary Market and Mortgage Insurance

Lenders recycle their money. One month they lend dollars by creating a mortgage. The next month they sell that mortgage. This process allows them to lend the same dollars the following month.

Most of these mortgages are ultimately aggregated into a Mortgage-Backed Security and then sold to investors in various forms. Monthly mortgage payments flow from borrowers through the servicers to MBS investors.

Not all MBS investors want to share in the same risks. The return of their capital is paramount to some above a desired return on their investment. Securitization of these cash flows allows the risks of each loan to be distributed among many participants. This additional marketability to many investors provides the liquidity to lenders allowing them to originate another mortgage to the next consumer.

Mortgage loans can be characterized into four categories based in part on their risk to investors. These four mortgage categories are Government, Agency, non-QM, and hard money loans. On the surface, the interest rate to borrowers increases in that order as the risk to investors rise. However, the credit risk of the loan does not necessarily rise in that order.

To understand this is to realize that Government and Agency loans are subsidized the federal government. These loans are securitized by a Government Sponsored Enterprise or GSE who guarantee the return of principal to all investors. Non-qualified mortgages [non-QM] are strictly financed by the capital markets where principal losses can be distributed through a credit waterfall structure assigning losses in a tiered manner first to investors who receive a higher return on their investment for accepting more risk. Hard money loans may be sold into a securitization but are more often thought to be sold directly to investors or retained by lenders who assume all or some degree of risk for each loan.

Government loans are securitized by the Government National Mortgage Association [Ginnie Mae or GNMA], a GSE within the Department of Housing and Urban Development [HUD]. Also within HUD is the Federal Housing Authority or FHA which absorbs credit losses on loans underwritten to their standards guaranteeing investors won't suffer losses. In addition to their well-known FHA program are the Indian Housing Loan Guarantee Program and Home Equity Conversion Mortgages [HECM], more prevalently known as reverse mortgages. The Department of Veterans Affairs guarantees VA loans. And the Department of Agriculture covers any losses on USDA loans.

The government guarantee of these loans allows the securitizations to be sold into the secondary market at a higher price and lower yield as they shield the risk of credit losses from investors. Therefore, the interest rate is lower than most non-government programs. The guarantee isn't wholly sponsored by taxpayer money. In addition to the interest rate these programs almost always charge the borrower fees based on the loan amount to offset the credit risk.

The VA charges the VA Funding Fee that varies depending on usage. But veterans who receive disability compensation of any amount are exempt from the funding fee. Despite the fee if required, the low rate and ability to finance 100% of the property value often make VA loans the cheapest way to finance a primary residence.

On most FHA mortgages there is an initial fee and a monthly fee based on the loan amount. An FHA loan incurs the Up Front Mortgage Insurance Premium or UFMIP. The fee is currently a hefty 1.75% of the loan amount on a purchase. This charge is commonly financed and added to the loan amount. Therefore, when a home buyer provides a downpayment of 5%, their equity is immediately diminished to 3.25%.

Additionally, they incur an annual mortgage insurance premium or MIP of 0.50% or as high as 0.75% depending on the amount and loan-to-value for loans with a term greater than 15 years. An annual

MIP of 0.55% is paid on all regular FHA loans that are refinanced. This increase in the monthly payment remains for at least 11 years or the life of the loan. (hud.gov, 2023)

These distinctions are notable because on Agency or conventional loans, private mortgage insurance or PMI is required only on mortgages when the loan-to-value is greater than 80%. The private mortgage insurance can be less than the FHA MIP rate when credit scores are excellent and the DTI is low. And on an Agency loan, when the LTV falls to less than 78%, the private mortgage insurance is automatically cancelled and no longer part of the mortgage payment. However, on FHA loans, again, that MIP is usually sticky for at least 11 years. The only other way it goes away is if a mortgage is paid off or refinanced out of an FHA program. Yet another distinction is that with an Agency loan, no Up Front Mortgage Insurance is charged. For these reasons, Agency loans are often preferable to FHA loans especially with borrowers who have credit scores near or above 700.

It also important to choose the way that mortgage insurance is paid on an Agency loan. Private mortgage insurance companies typically offer three different types of payment options. The most common is a separate item charged monthly to the borrower as a percentage of the loan amount, Borrower Paid Mortgage Insurance [BPMI]. This functions similarly to an additional interest rate just as the MIP of an FHA loan. As a simple example, one might have a 6.00% mortgage rate and a 1.00% private mortgage insurance rate, for a total annual rate of 7.00%. The second option is to pay a fixed dollar amount in advance that reduces or replaces the percentage required in the first option. The payment of that cost could be provided through a seller concession or other source. A third option is to have the cost implied in the rate rather than as a separate item, known as Lender Paid Mortgage Insurance [LPMI]. These are all usually available from the lender and should be presented by the mortgage loan originator. However, only BPMI is regularly presented to borrowers while the other two options are often overlooked. They really should each be analyzed for their impact on total cost for the planned horizon of the loan.

And to be clear, none of this particular mortgage insurance is for the benefit of the borrower. The benefit is paid to the investor to protect them from credit losses in the event of a default. The lender will obtain the PMI from one of several private mortgage insurance companies that will independently and competitively provide a rate determined by the final loan characteristics.

Conventional loans are underwritten according to the other two GSEs, the Federal National Mortgage Association [Fannie Mae or FNMA] and the Federal Home Loan Mortgage Corporation [Freddie Mac or FHLMC]. These are Agencies of the Executive Branch and also backed by the full faith and credit of the US Government. Thus, Agency mortgages imply no credit risk to investors. Once again, potential credit losses are not wholly subsidized by the government as home loans that exceed 80% of loan-to-value require an additional payment of private mortgage insurance.

The third credit tier was once referred to as non-Agency loans which consisted of Prime, Sub-Prime and Alt-A loans. These are now called non-Qualified Mortgages or non-QM. As the name implies, they are meant for borrowers who do not qualify for a government or agency loan for one reason or another yet might still be perceived as fairly non-risky loans. A perfect example are jumbo loans. Loan amounts over the maximum limit for a conventional loan fall into this category. For instance, a borrower providing a down payment of 50% on a $3 million home, who has excellent credit and a DTI of less than 25% would easily qualify for a non-QM loan with a rate that may be better than many conventional loans. Non-QM lenders typically do not charge any type of mortgage insurance although for loans over 80% this might be implied in the interest rate as if it were covered with LPMI.

Last and least favored are hard money loans that might be available to borrowers who don't qualify for the first three tiers of product. Hard money lenders often charge an initial fee, usually from 1 to 3% much in the same way that the FHA charges the Up Front Mortgage Insurance Premium. Their annual rates tend to be considerably higher than the previously discussed options, perhaps 2 to 5% more than a non-QM loan. They may be appropriate for short term financing under certain circumstances, are often used by investors with a different strategy or a unique opportunity that demands a very fast closing. By and large these would be considered a last resort for someone looking to purchase a primary residence.

23.   Loan Level Price Adjustments

Loan Level Price Adjustments [LLPAs] pertain to the individual risk factors identified for any mortgage loan. These can be more easily understood by separating them into four categories:

a. Purpose
b. Loan-to-Value [LTV]
c. Credit score [FICO]
d. Property

These four categories all function in combination with each other and to varying degrees. In other words, they are not considered independently of each other although when certain thresholds are met then other characteristics become less important or even of no importance. The opposite can be true, too. For instance, with a higher LTV or lower FICO, then adjustments for other factors become greater. And when a loan has both a high LTV and low FICO score, then the rate increase is amplified to an even greater extent with any other negative characteristic. Understanding the correlation between these risk factors and the interest rate is important.

It can be very helpful in preparation for financing a home so that each borrower is able to take advantage of an interest rate that makes the payment affordable. Otherwise, it may discourage home ownership as the rate effect on the mortgage payment may dictate that renting is a cheaper option.

These pricing adjustments change from time to time for FNMA and FHLMC and can change at any time for non-QM lenders at their discretion. This is typically dictated by investor sentiment among other things like the health of the real estate market. In a soft real estate market, LTV may have more of an impact on rate. Whereas in a thriving economy with low unemployment and higher wage gains, it is plausible that credit scores may have more subtle drifts in rate adjustments. But overall, FICO and LTV are the two main components that will influence the rate offered to one borrower and not their neighbor.

a. Purpose

There are three reasons to create a new mortgage. The purpose can be to purchase a home, refinance the interest rate, or convert equity into cash. This is more commonly referred to as "product type." Each of these are understood to have a different degree of risk. While FHA, VA, and USDA loans are not thought of as having loan level price adjustments, they do incur different fees or mortgage insurance based on the purpose of the loan. Otherwise, they are not subject to a rate variance based on any of these factors.

Agency, non-QM and hard money loans overtly have loan level price adjustments on all four categories. As the loan level price adjustments imply, purchase money loans are considered less risky than a simple rate and term refinance. While cash-out refinances are riskier yet. Because the homeowner equity is being reduced, they have less skin in the game than their current situation. Or investors may theorize any number of reasons why a higher rate may be warranted. For instance, thinking that the cash required by the borrower may be an indication of mismanaging money when the purpose of the cash is for debt consolidation. Whether each individual loan scenario may justify the increase in rate pursuant to the cash-out characteristic is not considered.

One could argue that refinancing from a purchase mortgage just to get a lower rate and payment, without taking any cash-out, shows strong money management skills by the borrower. Right or wrong, the purchase rate is still often though not always lower than the rate for a simple refinance. As an example, all else being equal, the rate on a single-family residence for a borrower with a 700 FICO at 75% LTV might get a 6.000% rate on a purchase mortgage, 6.250% on a rate refinance, and 6.875% on a cash-out refinance.

An owelty loan is an exception to the cash-out refinance rate adjustment. This is actually a cash-out refinance but for the express purpose of the entire proceeds being provided to an ex-spouse as required by a divorce decree. It serves the purpose of satisfying the decree obligation and also removes the ex-spouse from the deed by way of a quit-claim deed where they relinquish their interest in the property.

b. Loan-to-Value

Loan-to-value, [LTV], is always recognized as the percentage of the home value. So, a $600,000 loan on a $1,000,000 home would be a 60% LTV loan. Conventional wisdom suggests that an 80% LTV provides the best loan with the lowest rate and should be the goal of all homebuyers. This is false more often than true.

Apart from US Treasury yields, the factor with the most bearing on a mortgage rate is the LTV. This deals with the previously mentioned primary concern of the investor or lender which is getting their money back or being made whole on the original loan balance. And to be candid, this boils down to whether or not the net proceeds from a foreclosure will be equal to or less than the loan amount.

Generally speaking, and with regard to home values above $300,000, at a 60% LTV or lower, the probability of the investor taking any losses is just about nil. Therefore, the rate will be about the same regardless of credit score, the second main factor, or most other elements. At each 5% to 10% increment above 60%, the rate will normally increase. And it will continue to increase ever more severely the worse the credit score and the higher the LTV.

Between 75% and 80%, the risk is the highest. Counterintuitively, conventional loans between 80% and 85% LTV may have a slightly improved rate. This is because those loans will require private mortgage insurance [PMI] covering the investor from losses but still with adequate borrower's equity to keep them opposed to a default. However, the cost of PMI will also be highly dependent on the credit score of the borrower(s). The higher the credit score, the lower cost of PMI and vice versa.

Hypothetically speaking, two borrowers with very high credit scores may often want to consider leveraging up to a 95% LTV. If the interest rate only increases by 0.50% and the PMI is only 0.25%, then tying up an additional 15.00% to only save 0.75% might be worth reconsidering. That 15% may be better used to buy a cash flow positive investment property or other income producing asset.

For instance, consider the purchase of a $625,000 house and a borrower having a 740 credit score or higher. A $500,000 mortgage at 5.00% would require a monthly payment just under $2,700 along with the down payment of $125,000. A $593,750 mortgage might be offered with a mortgage rate also at 5.00% coupled with a buyout of the PMI of $10,000. That payment would amount be about $3,200 monthly for an annual payment difference of $6,000. But the down payment would only be $31,250 along with the $10,000 leaving the borrower with $83,750 in cash. If this money can be invested and earn more than the payment difference of 6,000 annually, greater than about 7.20%, this ought to be considered.

On the contrary, a higher down payment is likely advisable in proportion to the worse a borrower's credit score. The financing costs work to their disadvantage. This is why it is typically recommended to improve credit scores as much as possible before buying or refinancing. This allows consumers to take advantage of the leverage provided by a higher LTV. A better credit score provides a borrower far more benefit than a higher down payment.

Separately, a VA loan at 100% LTV oftentimes provides the lowest mortgage rate available. And in that case, provided the payment is affordable, why tie up any cash at all on a down payment? That 20% may also be better used to buy a cash flow positive investment property or a boat. But a good rental property would certainly be more fiscally responsible.

c. Credit Score

Mortgage underwriting guidelines from virtually all lenders require a full credit report to be obtained from the three main credit bureaus, Equifax, Experian and TransUnion. The merged report provides details on current and past debt obligations along with their payment histories and other pertinent credit data. Other revealing information such as financial judgements, tax liens, and credit inquiries or requests for lines of credit are also observed. In sum, those three bureaus each provide their own credit score. That score is basically their measure of a person's historical ability to manage debt and their intent to repay debt.

What is important to recognize is that each borrower must have an established history of credit use in order for the bureaus to provide a credit score. And they must have credit scores reported from all three bureaus in order to get a mortgage. Additionally, this minimum history required by most lenders is generally considered to be three open lines of credit going back twelve months (3 x 12) or two open lines aged at least twenty-four months (2 x 24).

Please understand that no one is advocating that a balance is carried on any lines of credit to meet the history qualification. It's best not to have any debt. But those lines of credit must be available even if they are all just $200 credit limits. And the longer those credit lines are open, the higher the potential for the credit score. Avoid closing them when possible.

The bureaus have progressively made it easier to understand how to increase credit scores and there are many tools and credit repair companies to help in this endeavor. One might benefit from knowing there are different types credit reports and scores such as a consumer credit score which is what may be provided from a bank or credit card app. As a note of caution, that score might be considerably higher or lower than the scores obtained by a mortgage company from the same credit bureaus.

Of the three scores, the middle score is what will be used to determine the mortgage interest rate. Although it is written that consumers can get a mortgage with a credit score below 620, favorable interest rates will be found with scores nearer or above 700. 680 is generally a threshold where rates become palatable. Above 720 will gain access to much lower rates. And when borrowing more than 80% of the home value, private mortgage insurance will be more tolerable. Each lender will be different in where they adjust the rate and by how much as it is up to their discretion. Generally, though, the breakpoints are at every 20-point intervals.

When permission has been provided to a mortgage loan originator to pull a credit report, the consumer has 45 days to allow other lenders to do the same without any negative impact on the scores. (Consumer Financial Protection Bureau, 2023) And to be fair, borrowers probably should do so just to keep everyone honest and make sure they are obtaining a competitive rate. That said, rates can and do often change each day, sometimes multiple times each day. And although they might be made to sound the same, slight variations in the Loan Estimate may exhibit deceptive differences in interest rates. And sometimes, people just make honest mistakes. So, compare apples to apples with someone who can spot the difference between types of apples, which is usually somebody with a lot of experience and who instinctually seems trustworthy.

Probably most important of all, lenders will continue to monitor the borrower's credit report throughout the origination process up until closing. So, it is extremely important not to do anything that may negatively impact the original score, like applying for a new credit card or even using a credit card to buy furniture for the new home, until after the loan has funded and the keys are in hand to that home.

d. Property

A borrower's primary residence is thought to be the least risky of all property types. A family needs a roof over their head. But they don't need two or three. And therefore, it should be expected that the interest rate on a second or third or fourth home (actually to be classified as another second home) is considerably higher than that of a primary residence. In the eyes of FNMA, the interest price adjustment is the same for a second home as it is for an investment property.

Whether it is declared as a second home or investment property, the opportunity may arise for it be rented. Logically, this rent would produce income that could pay or at least supplement the monthly payments required by the mortgage. This may be necessary or not but that is not taken into consideration with regard to the interest rate adjustment.

The thought process is that a borrower will first default on their second home(s) or investment properties before they fail to make the payment on the primary home's mortgage. The borrower will put family first. If their finances became stressed to such a point where they had to choose which mortgage payment to make, they would likely choose to use rental income from an investment property to pay the mortgage on their own home. Thus, the probability and actual experience has been that delinquency and defaults on investment properties are higher than on primary residences. And, therefore, with the higher risk assumed by the utility of the property, the investor demands a higher interest rate.

To a far lesser degree and for different reasons, there are loan-level price adjustments on condos, 2, 3, and 4-unit properties and manufactured homes. All four share one similar trait in that they are in less demand. With a smaller market of buyers, any price depreciation in an economic downturn might be more dramatic.

Although duplexes, triplexes and quadplexes are highly sought after by investors, they still may suffer more negative price shock in a collapsing housing market. A weak economy and/or weak labor market would infer falling rental prices and/or higher vacancy rates. A 1–4-unit property may be purchased as a primary residence. In this scenario, it would not incur the significant price adjustment of an investment property, but only about 1/5th of the rate increase based on it being a multi-family home. (Selling Guide, 2024)

Any property with 5 units or more would not be eligible for a conventional residential loan underwritten by FNMA or FHLMC. However, these government agencies do sponsor financing programs specifically for multi-unit properties of this size or greater. Additionally, under certain real estate market conditions, non-QM lenders may be willing to provide financing for 5- to 8-unit properties.

24.   Prepayment Penalty Period

Prepayment penalties are designed to protect the investor from interest rate risk. If an investor buys a mortgage with a coupon of 6%, they will do so expecting to receive those amortized principal and interest cash flows each month for a certain period of time. Should interest rates fall in the near term and the mortgage be repaid prematurely, their reinvestment of that capital will now be subject to the lower yields of that lower interest rate environment.

Contrarily, should interest rates rise significantly then curtailments and full repayments would be expected to slow dramatically. With this lack of prepayments, the investor now may be holding that 6% coupon for a far longer period of time than normally expected preventing redeployment of that tied-up capital at those higher future market yields. And the market value of that asset also declines as rates rise posing another source of pain for the investor.

Understand that the borrower and investor have diametrically opposed positions on directional changes in interest rates. When mortgage rates fall the borrower may benefit by refinancing but the investor has to reinvest their capital at a currently lower market rate.

This prepayment risk is extremely problematic for MBS investors. Wall Street employs nuclear engineers and rocket scientists, literally, to produce research on prepayment trends to aid institutional investors' analysis of this potential dilemma and satisfy sales.

Government and Agency residential mortgage underwriting standards have prohibited prepayment penalties on all loans since 2014. State laws also often forbid any provision in the promissory note that would require a prepayment penalty on mortgages for primary and secondary residences of the homeowner. These state lending laws are designed to protect consumers with regard to lending practices.

However, commercial loans for investment properties of one to any number of units are outside the scope of these laws in many states. In these instances, the borrower may certify the property is to be used solely for commercial purposes and they themselves will never occupy the house at any time while the mortgage is outstanding. By doing so, the mortgage is considered a business loan.

Non-QM and hard money lenders underwrite some mortgages on 1–4-unit residential investment properties where a prepayment penalty may be applied. In particular, DSCR loans are viewed as commercial loans at least in part because the ability to repay is entirely exclusive of the borrower's means. Rather, the property's ability to generate income through rental payments is the only consideration for repayment. By this standard, the borrower's ability to repay a mortgage on their homestead or vacation home is not impaired.

The prepayment penalty amount may vary from lender to lender at their discretion as conveyed in their own underwriting guidelines. The penalty may apply to partial repayments above a certain percentage of the monthly scheduled principal payment amount. On a full repayment, the calculation to determine the penalty will typically be based on the outstanding loan balance at the time of the prepayment. The penalty may be a few months or an entire year of interest on the outstanding balance, or it may be a fixed percentage, like three or five percent. These details are crucial to determining the following option the borrower may choose.

The standard prepayment penalty period is three years but may range from zero to five years at the option of the borrower when offered by the lender. The shorter the period that the mortgage is subject to a prepayment penalty then the higher the offered rate will be. The longer the prepayment penalty, the lower the interest rate. The investor is willing to reduce their yield in exchange for the protection against prepayment risk. Investors prefer more certainty.

When market rates are higher than average, it could prove worthwhile to consider a shorter prepayment period. Paying a slightly higher rate in the near term may provide a greater opportunity to refinance even with only marginally lower rates. Choosing the lowest rate as a consequence of the longest penalty period would require inclusion of the penalty amount when considering to refinance. Theoretically, the decrease in interest rates would need to be greater in this scenario.

This concept aligns with a decision to be discussed in Chapter 26. Deciding to pay discount points for a lower rate would be a strategy in conflict with accepting a higher rate to remove the prepayment penalty. Rate options ought to be in alignment with, among other things, financing objectives and interest rate cycles.

25. Lender or Borrower Paid Commission

There are three distinct types of loan origination channels: 1. commercial banks and credit unions; 2. mortgage banks and lenders; and, 3. mortgage brokers. Regardless of this, most all loans will be sold into the capital markets, securitized, and sold to investors. Fundamentally, these investors dictate the general interest rate.

And like any industry, there are incremental price increases at each point of refinement from the natural resource to the end product. In the mortgage industry, the mortgage is the natural resource and Mortgage-Backed Securities are the finished product. Or, similarly, many mortgages land in derivatives like CMOs or other structured products and sold to more sophisticated investors.

In that vein, the first two loan origination channels generally use their own capital or warehouse lines of credit to fund each loan, whereas, mortgage brokers do not. For that reason, commercial banks and mortgage banks do not disclose the revenue generated for them by each loan transaction. Nor is the loan originator able to negotiate the interest rate with the borrower. The interest rates are set by the company.

Although infrequent and at the discretion of the company not the originator, there may be a very small "pricing concession" or rate cost decrease provided to a borrower to compensate for a delay or other material harm incurred at the fault of the company. But this is rare and should not be expected, and probably is not worth seeking.

Working with a mortgage broker may offer at least one advantage when it comes to the interest rate. Mortgage brokers have the option of offering the interest rate to the borrower with or without disclosing their commission or compensation to the borrower. As the name implies, with borrower paid commission the amount of compensation to be paid to the mortgage broker will be clearly stated as a separate line item on the loan documents. This is where an advantage may be gained for the borrower.

That advantage is not in regard to negotiating the commission to be provided to the mortgage broker. Keep in mind, the mortgage broker has expenses just like the commercial bank and mortgage lender. They have costs associated with the time, energy and materials required to produce each loan including paying the loan originator.

At the same time, these costs are not shouldered or incurred by the commercial bank or mortgage lender. And that is why the mortgage broker is able to obtain a wholesale interest rate from the bank or lender whom will fund and acquire the loan if only temporarily.

When the borrower compensates the mortgage broker directly within the transaction via borrower paid commission, the wholesale interest rate is passed on directly to the borrower. Therein lies the advantage. In effect, the borrower is paying a one-time fee to procure the loan which comes at a lower interest rate.

Otherwise, with lender paid commission, the compensation to the originator as well as any profit generated from the production of the loan is imbedded in the interest rate. In other words, whether the mortgage is obtained from a bank, lender or broker channel, the interest rate provided includes the compensation paid by the borrower. From one point of view, this cost is not outrightly disclosed and in some sense could be construed as hidden when it is baked into the interest rate rather than as "borrower paid commission."

This could be an advantage or a disadvantage to the borrower. The difference will normally depend on the amount of time the loan is outstanding. This is a mortgage strategy well worth consideration.

Strictly as an example, to make the math easy and with all else being equal, a loan with borrower paid commission of 2.50% might provide an interest rate of 5.00%; whereas, with lender paid commission, the rate may be 5.50%. Therefore, after approximately five years, the 5.00% rate would hold the advantage or be "in the money," so to speak. But if that loan were to be refinanced or paid off through the sale of the home or by any other means, then the 5.50% rate would have cost the borrower less money. With consideration to the 2.50% possibly being financed into the loan, at some point beyond five years and thereafter, the borrower would very likely have been better off with the lower rate. Notably, that math can be easily calculated. But the uncertainty of outside variables may influence the expected horizon of the loan repayment.

26.   Discount, Par or Premium Pricing

Perhaps the most important and final decision that a borrower must make is to choose the interest rate. Yes, the borrower has a choice. And this is where borrowers are least informed. That is to say, they are provided with the least amount of information and education about their options. And at this very moment is when borrowers' future wealth may be impacted the most.

When a borrower issues a mortgage, most of the time they may choose between discount, par or premium pricing. And that ought to matter to consumers. In the bond market, fortunes and careers are made or lost on these decisions.

Par is bond parlance for 100. This can be more easily thought of as 100% of the face value of the obligation per $100.00 of borrowed capital. The par value of a bond is 100 when the coupon rate and the yield to maturity are the exact same. (Fabozzi, Fixed Income Mathematics, 1993, 1997)

As an example, let's say the US Treasury issues new Ten-Year Notes with a 5.00% coupon rate this month. At the exact moment they are auctioned to buyers, last month's issuance of Ten-Year Notes, having also been issued with a 5.00% coupon, are trading at a yield of 5.13%. This is equivalent to a price of $98.99 per $100.00 of investment capital. The new Ten-Year Notes would be sold at $99.00. It is marginally higher due to the extra month of interest. Remember with bonds, when the yield goes up, the price goes down because the coupon or interest income provided remains the same.

Conversely, when the yield goes down, the price goes up. Therefore, if the Treasury decided to issue the notes with a coupon of 5.25% with the when-issued note yielding 5.13%, this higher coupon would fetch a market price of $100.93 and the yield on the new note would be relative to the existing notes of similar maturity.

Note well that "a point" is one percent of the loan amount, where $99 and $101 would be considered one full discount point or premium point, respectively. A "point" does not refer to the difference in coupon rate or interest rate, such as 4.00% or 5.00%.

After consideration for all of the aforementioned factors in this chapter regarding what will determine the interest rate, a range of rates may be provided to choose from the lowest to the highest rate available.

As per the Treasury Note example above, there will rarely be a single rate offered exactly at par. But there will normally be a rate just slightly above or below par. This may be thought of as the safest bet for most consumers. But those situations are probably quite limited and would likely result in leaving a lot of money on the table. There are likely more numerous situations when taking a different approach may be more appropriate and actually limit risk.

Most consumers may be more familiar with paying discount points in order to "buy down" the interest rate. It is quite common for lenders to offer this to consumers who are naturally attracted to a lower mortgage rate as it will provide a lower required monthly payment.

The math on this choice is generally quite clear in a refinance but slightly less so on purchase mortgage. When refinancing, the dollar amount paid for the lower rate is typically financed. Whereas, with a purchase, this amount required to obtain the lower rate is generally additional money the home buyer would need to provide to complete the transaction. Bear in mind this additional money might instead be used to increase the downpayment thus providing more equity for a lower LTV and thus a smaller loan and decreased payment. There are numerous tradeoffs to consider which add to the importance of having a unified mortgage management strategy.

The required monthly principal & interest payment on a 30-year level pay mortgage of $100,000 with a fixed rate of 6.000% is $599.60. Let's imagine it cost $1,000 to reduce an interest rate from 6.000% to 5.625%. And this $1,000 is financed or added to the loan amount such that the payment on $101,000 at 5.625% is $581.40.

The difference between monthly payments is $18.20. It may often seem appealing to have this lower payment.

In simple terms, the cost of $1,000 divided by the lower payment of $18.20 per month implies the borrower will actually begin to save money due to the lower rate beginning in month 56. If the borrower were to refinance or sell the home prior to month 56 of the mortgage, then this would be a losing proposition.

And it is also true that over the course of 360 months, the lower rate would mean a savings in total payments of $6,529.52. This math is quite simple to calculate. 360 payments of $599.60 equals $215,838.19 versus 360 x $581.40 = $209,308.67. That is a significant savings compared to the theoretical $1,000 to obtain the lower interest rate.

Critical, though, to understand is that the average life of a mortgage in the mortgage universe has historically averaged only between five and six years. The mortgage market knows this and efficiently prices the option to buy down the interest rate accordingly. The odds tend to favor the casino.

Most consumers are taught to expect to have their mortgage for 30 years, because, well, it is a 30-year mortgage after all. But rarely does anyone actually make the 360th payment on their mortgage. Traditionally, the three "Ds" said properly only in a Bronx accent, death, divorce, and de job are what make this true.

So, it is with caution one should proceed in paying additional money in advance to buy down the interest rate, most especially when borrowed or financed into the closing costs as is usually the case with a refinance. This results in diminishing the equity for the homeowner until that breakeven month is reached. It may be worth noting that, in close examination of the amortization schedules, it is not until month 117 when the loan balance is less on the $101,000 loan at 5.625% than the $100,000 loan at 6.000%. However, that completely disregards the aggregate savings in monthly loan payments which when factored into consideration takes one back to break even at month 56 as previously suggested. This is a difference in analytical perspective between the importance or difference between cash flow and equity.

From one perspective, including perhaps that of the IRS, buying down the interest rate is effectively paying that interest in advance to the lender. As the tax code is subject to change and a professional tax advisor's counsel should be sought in this regard for timely guidance, discount points may be tax deductible on the same line item as the mortgage interest expense. Call it what you want, but the lender gets the money that you would otherwise being paying out over the course of several months, prior to that breakeven point where the lower payment has eclipsed this sum paid up front. From a lender's point of view, any amount received in advance decreases the amount of potential future losses that remain. Interest on a loan is payment for risk of the loan not being repaid.

The point remains that despite one's plans and best intentions, it is not always a winning strategy to buy down the interest rate. The reduction of payment must at some point exceed the cost paid in advance or financed. Then, each month thereafter, the strategy produces an increasingly positive result. On a home financing where the plan is to retain the house, for primary use or rental, this is a winning strategy. But this may be truer when rates are at low points in interest rate cycles. And when rates are higher than average historical levels, then it could turn out to be a wasteful maneuver.

There are situations where the opposite is true and accepting a higher rate above par can be a better strategy. There is one time when this is most often true, which is when purchasing a home. And there is a second time when this almost always true, while refinancing. In both instances, there is little downside if future rates were to rise. There is little harm if rates remain the same. And there is plenty of upside if rates fall.

Recalling the Ten-Year US Treasury example, a rate above par is when the issuer sells a note to the market with a coupon above the prevailing rate for a similar loan. The Treasury gets the additional money but pays a higher rate for the life of the loan.

The borrower can achieve the same outcome when issuing a mortgage, too. The net effect is to receive money at closing that will be applied to reduce some if not all of the closing costs associated with the transaction. This will be provided as a "lender credit" on the loan estimates and closing documentation.

Previously, our mortgage example was this:

The required monthly principal & interest payment on a 30-year level pay mortgage of $100,000 with a fixed rate of 6.000% is $599.60. Let's imagine it cost $1,000 to reduce an interest rate from 6.000% to 5.625%. And that $1,000 is financed or added to the loan amount such that the payment on $101,000 at 5.625% is $581.40.

Hypothetically, a lender may also be able to offer a rate 6.375% and provide a lender credit of $1,000 per $100,000. In this instance, the loan amount remains $100,000 and the borrower accepts a higher interest rate of 6.375% where the payment is $623.87.

These two divergent scenarios may be more easily conceived by studying the rate stack provided in Exhibit 26-1.

Assume for a moment that a person is buying a $125,000 home and wants to finance only $100,000 to maintain a loan-to-value of 80% to avoid paying private mortgage insurance.

Typically, there are legal and other costs associated with producing the mortgage which the borrower is obligated to pay. If those were to amount to $1,000, then the borrower may choose to take the higher rate of 6.375% in order to receive the $1.000 lender credit. Therefore, the borrower would only need to meet the $25,000 down payment amount to complete the transaction and not bring the additional $1,000.

Perhaps the borrower does not have the additional $1,000, would prefer to use the cash for home furnishings rather than pay for those with a credit card at a rate multiple times higher, or they believe that money could be invested elsewhere and yield greater than 6.375%.

Exhibit 26-1

Rate	Price	Amount Per $100,000	P&I Payment
5.500%	$98.875	-$1,250.00	$567.79
5.625%	$99.000	-$1.000.00	$575.66
5.750%	$99.375	-$625.00	$583.57
5.875%	$99.750	-$250.00	$591.54
6.000%	$100.000	+/- $0.00	$599.60
6.125%	$100.250	+250.00	$607.61
6.250%	$100.625	+$625.00	$615.72
6.375%	$101.000	+$1,000.00	$623.87
6.500%	$101.250	+$1,250.00	$632.07
6.625%	$101.500	+$1,500.00	$640.31

All are possible, potentially valid reasons, and often quite common. Mortgage interest rates and the required monthly payment tend to both be lower than any other financing options available to consumers. So, the opportunity cost of spending or generating this cash should be considered.

It is important to recognize that laws restrict the use of the lender credit. It cannot be applied to the borrower's equity in the home. In other words, those monies are not permitted to be used as part of the borrower's down payment on a purchase nor to reduce the principal loan balance on a refinance.

Compare the possibilities between a lender credit and paying points with cash on a purchase transaction. If a borrower were enticed into selecting the lower interest rate of 5.625%, the savings would not be immediate. Not only did the transaction cost $1,000, but the additional cost of buying down the rate, paying $1,000 in "discount points" would also first need to be recaptured prior to obtaining the benefit of the lower rate. With a difference in payment of $48.21, it would take the borrower with the lower rate 42 months to recover the $2,000 outlay.

And a lot can happen in three and a half years. What if rates were to fall dramatically, well below 5.625%? How low would they have to go to justify foregoing the sunk cost of previously buying down the rate? If rates went to 5.00% after one year, would the same borrower again consider buying down the rate to 4.25%?

A "no-cost loan" is one in which all the transactions costs incurred with completing the mortgage are paid for by a lender credit, or at least in part by a lender credit. In this option, there would need to be a large enough lender credit to cover these costs.

Assume a borrower has $100,000 remaining principal balance financed at 6.500% and it will cost $1,000 in refinance transaction costs. With consideration of the rate table above, the borrower would do no harm by refinancing at 6.375%. The cost to do so would be zero because the lender credit will cover the expense of refinancing. In the very first month of the new mortgage the benefit would be captured and accumulate each month thereafter. In utilizing this methodology, it is extremely important to maintain the same number of remaining months on the mortgage. Extending the amortization term back out to 30 years might provide a lower payment but cost more in the long run. Multiplying the new payment times the new number of payments ought to be less than the current payment multiplied by the remaining number of payments. In these instances, where the term is not being extended, no money is brought to the closing, and the new payment is less, it is almost certainly advantageous to refinance regardless of how much lower that payment might be.

As a common-sense loan originator used to suggest to customers, "If you were going out to your mailbox and saw a fifty-dollar bill on the sidewalk would you bend down and pick it up? What if you knew another fifty-dollar bill was going to be at that same spot on the sidewalk every month. Would you make a habit of picking it up? What if I could pay your phone bill every month? People switch phone companies to save $15 a month. I see the TV commercials. Why wouldn't you want to refinance to save $50 every month? What sense does that make?"

Other than with a no-cost loan, the basic assumption and common practice on a refinance is for the discount points and transaction costs to be financed. Continuing with the same assumptions, this would result in increasing the balance of the loan with the lower rate to $102,000 and thus slightly increasing the payment to $587.17 from that displayed on the rate table.

Isolating the two options, the payment on the no-cost loan afforded by the "lender credit" is $623.87 versus the additional $2,000 loan's payment of $587.17. The difference in payment is $36.70. Where $2,000 divided by $36.70 is 55, the number of months until the borrower with the lower rate of 5.625% has a net benefit from selecting the lower rate. Meanwhile, the borrower with the higher rate has a lower initial loan balance, therefore more equity and less to lose should they find themselves in position where they were required to sell the property. Additionally, as suggested before, should rates fall, the borrower with the higher rate would require a less significant drop in interest rates to gain an advantage by refinancing as well as a lower balance to refinance.

One theory relied upon by regulators and often considered to be conventional wisdom stipulates that the borrower must recoup the cost associated with refinancing within 2 to 3 years. For instance, if the borrower had a current rate of 6.625% and a payment of $640.31, the 5.625% loan would produce a payment of $575.66 for a difference of $64.65. The theoretical refinance cost of $2,000 would be recovered by month 31 making this an acceptable loan. But not until month 42 would the lower rate be providing a cost savings advantage superior to the no-cost loan.

This shows that when refinancing, the current mortgage rate must also be considered into the calculation. This also demonstrates how it is arguably an easy decision to receive a higher rate and take the lender credit when refinancing a mortgage. Although it initially sounds counter-intuitive to accept a higher rate when refinancing, what is being suggested is that this higher rate is still lower than the interest rate on the current mortgage. The application of this strategy makes financing decisions nearly riskless with regard to when to refinance. Should rates fall further, refinancing again at no cost might be an option. Should rates go up or remain the same, fine. The refinanced rate is still lower than the rate previously held.

It is just as tough to pick the bottom as it is to pick the top of any market. Having a higher balance and lower rate actually reduces the opportunities to refinance. And therefore, it would be considered a conservative bet to lay out less money or not add transaction costs and discount points to the remaining principal balance in order to seek the lowest available rate. Rates may go lower.

Make Your Mortgage Matter

27. Rate Lock Period and Extensions

The final, least discussed and most loathed of all mortgage loan originator conversations, when necessary, is the cost to extend the rate lock period prior to closing.

Be very aware that the rate quoted in initial discussions with a loan originator, shown on a Loan Estimate, or even the rate that is locked may change if any of the aforementioned loan details change. When all of these loan parameters have been established and verified, the final rate will be determined. Whenever the borrower chooses to do so, what is actually being locked are the chosen lender's published rates at that moment in time which are then applicable to the final characteristics of the   loan.

Prior to locking in the rate schedule, it is subject to change due to market volatility. Broadly, interest rate markets are constantly changing. Most of the time, mortgage rates may change from day to day but not materially. In other words, although there may be subtle changes in the amount of lender credit or discount points per 1/8th of a point increment in rate, the par rate does not tend to move by 1/8th of a point on a daily basis. That 6.000% rate may be $100.056 one day and $100.128 the next. Only in less certain and more volatile markets would the par rate go from 6.00% to 5.875% or 6.125% in one day or even in one week.

But that can happen intraday, too. This might be true when a key economic indicator is released and be widely different than economists' estimates. And this does often happen but not regularly. As long as the Fed maintains their primary concern to be controlling inflation and unemployment, then the quarterly Consumer Price Index [CPI] and the Employment Situation Summary, referred to as the nonfarm employment data or simply nonfarm payrolls, usually released on the morning of the first Friday of each month, will have the most impact on bond rates. It is a good idea to take note of these two and other announcements when considering locking in the rate.

The mortgage rate is locked by the consumer to protect them from rates moving up. Once locked, the lender is exposed to that risk of interest rate volatility. When yields rise, bond prices fall. When the lender goes to sell that loan to the secondary market, they would potentially get less money than the amount they had expected.

Along with the specific rate, an interest rate lock period is also chosen at this time. The period can be 15, 30, 45 or really any number of days that any lender might choose to offer the borrower. The longer the lock period, the more expensive the rate. 6.000% at par may be offered for 30 days. But for 45 days, the cost may be $100.125, and 60 days may be $100.375.

The reason for the difference in price between lock period day count is based on the cost of the lender to hedge the mortgage rate against changes in the interest rate markets. The lender takes some risk in the cost of a hedge when they are not able to deliver a real loan. If they have chosen to employ a hedging strategy, they may be forced to sell or buy back a synthetic mortgage at whatever price the current market might offer, for a gain or loss.

For instance, if a $100,000 loan is locked at 6.000% for 30 days, the lender will normally be able to sell that loan in the following 45-to-75-day window. After the loan closes and all the paperwork and monies are reconciled, the lender is then able to deliver the loan back into the secondary market where it will be likely be securitized. If rates have moved up since that lock date, the lender would naturally receive less than $100,000.

In instances where there is a delay in closing past the initial lock period due to no fault of the lender, the borrower will be asked to pay a fee to extend the lock for another limited period of time. This cost may be arbitrary to the extent of being different from one lender to the next. But it is usually an established set of fees at each lender and, therefore, not different from one loan or borrower to the next for loans offered from that particular lender

One other important distinction between rate lock guidelines from one lender to the next is whether the lock must be valid through the closing date or the funding date. These dates are often the same on a purchase. But on a refinance of a primary residence, the borrower is afforded a 3 day right of rescission to review the paperwork and back out of the deal if they have an issue or for no reason at all but buyer's remorse.

Most lenders choose to prioritize purchase transactions over refinances. Purchases take precedence because they may involve one party to the transaction being left without a place to live for the night. Sellers may close on the sale of their current property and the purchase of their next home on the very same day. Whereas, the single party to a refinance is already the owner of that property.

Inevitably many purchase transaction closing dates are set for the last day of the month. This may be due to a first-time home buyer's rental agreement expiring at the end of the month. Or it may be due to the realtors' and/or loan originator's incentive to book their sales prior to month end so they receive their commission sooner rather than waiting a full 30 more days depending on their employers' payment structure.

Regardless of the reason, more loans close on the last day of the month than any other. This is a subtle factor that might be wise to evaluate when choosing how many days to lock in a rate. If it is the first day of the month, locking in the rate on a refinance for only 30 days ought to be considered a bit riskier than it would be for a purchase.

Providing all documentation in a timely manner is absurdly important. One day may seem immaterial at first. However, it may be that a lock period ends on a Friday and Monday is a holiday. That one day now amounts to four extra days, Saturday to Tuesday. Additionally, many lenders offer a minimum lock extension of seven days. Missing the expected closing date by just one day may in reality cost you seven.

Oftentimes, the cost of locking in a rate for 45 days as opposed to 30 days is marginally less than the cost of locking for 30 and extending for 15. This is worth exploring with the loan originator.

Sometimes there are unforeseen and/or unavoidable delays, such as repairs being required subsequent to findings in an appraisal. In most cases, the borrower has very little leverage and will be subject to such lock extension fees. This cost can ultimately be hundreds or thousands of dollars depending on the size of the loan and length of the delay in closing.

There are even worse potential outcomes. Some lenders may allow only two lock extensions. And once those have been used, the loan is likely subject to being re-locked at the current prevailing interest rate. So, if rate was locked for 30 days, twice extended for 7 days, so that now 45 days have elapsed, the interest rate could be dramatically higher to a point where the margin to refinance at a meaningfully lower rate has since evaporated.

Rather than extend the lock period the borrower may allow it to expire by intention or omission and with often worse repercussions. Bear in mind it is the responsibility of the borrower and not the loan originator or lender to manage the rate lock period. Under these circumstances, lenders might only offer the same or worst-case pricing. The borrower may have let the rate expire inadvertently when rates have risen. In this case, a lender will likely offer the current higher rate with a new lock.

When rates have fallen a borrower may let the lock period expire by design in an attempt to obtain a lower rate. Many lenders will require a 30-day waiting period before allowing the same consumer to lock in a new rate at better pricing. And at that point, the rate drop may have reversed and the prevailing market rate offered after the 30-day waiting period could be higher than the original rate. This can lead the borrower to take his business elsewhere. Rather than lose the deal, not all but some lenders allow a rate to "float down" to that lower market rate.

(Note Well: This is 3rd instance where "float" has a different meaning in the mortgage industry. A floating rate note is also called an adjustable-rate mortgage. Floating the rate is waiting to lock in the interest rate. And floating down the rate is when the lender provides a lower rate than the initial locked rate due to better market conditions.)

28.   Closing the Deal

Each loan file may eventually be assigned to a processor and underwriter who will work together to make sure the proper documentation and calculations are completed in the file to meet the investors requirements. All three people, the loan originator, processor, and underwriter should be very familiar with the underwriting guidelines and have a firm understanding of what documentation will be required. The documents needed will vary based on the many parameters of each loan. No two loan files are the same.

Oftentimes, documents are provided that may be insufficient to validate a specific requirement. This may necessitate more documentation to be requested from a borrower or third party. It is of great importance to each lender to have the exact proper documents in each and every file. Investors usually have the right to audit any file they choose. Files are sometimes chosen randomly to be audited. And if there is ever a delinquency or default of a loan, that fille will most definitely be reviewed.

There are two potential negative consequences for a lender having incomplete loan documentation on approved loans. Upon finding a file is lacking in substance, investors often have the recourse of returning that loan to the lender and getting their principal back. When a loan is delinquent or has defaulted, any losses on that loan would fall to the lender. But the lender is not in business for that risk. In other words, that may be highly detrimental to their bottom line.

Even worse, with numerous incomplete files, an investor or bank may withdraw the warehouse line of credit that the lender uses to fund loans, their primary source of liquidity prior to selling loans to the capital markets. This could put the lender out of business immediately. In very simple and general terms, this counterparty risk is what caused the collapse of Bear, Stearns & Co. in 2008.

Lenders are also subject to satisfying anti-money laundering regulations. These rules require lenders to verify the source of funds for all monies used in the transaction. Therefore, cash deposited into accounts are often excluded unless they were in the account several months prior. And when money is moved around from one bank account to another, multiple monthly statements from each account are likely to be required in order to track the source of those funds.

This is all to say that when a lender asks for a specific document from a consumer, this document is most likely going to be required at some point in order to complete the transaction, whether the borrower likes it or not. And it is pretty unreasonable to think that any skeletons in the closet will go unnoticed when being approved for a mortgage. There are multiple different tools that lenders use to make certain that the borrower's finances are what they appear to be and prevent any hint of mortgage fraud.

There are several reasons why a loan may be denied to a borrower despite an early conditional approval. The most common of these is a failure to document the ability to repay thresholds, such as the Debt-to-Income ratio. For instance, if an application represented that a borrower made $5,000 per month, but the paystubs and W2s result in proof of a lesser amount of $4,500, this difference may be a problem too significant to resolve by other means.

But there often may be different solutions to these types of issues. In a purchase, the solution may be for the borrower to provide a larger down payment thus decreasing the loan size and the resulting mortgage payment. In refinance transactions, this may be less solvable. For instance, a debt-consolidation transaction may be structured where all the cash-out may be necessary to pay off other monthly obligations so the only payment left is the mortgage. If the DTI still doesn't fall below the requirements, the deal may not be workable.

Operationally, lending departments typically work on a queue. Each underwriter may have dozens if not many more loans that stack up in their queue to review each day. Some are new, some might be resubmitted with most but not all conditions received, and some are in for final review perhaps for a third, fourth or fifth time. The time from start to finish on a loan may be as quick as just a few days although this is rare. And while most lenders are quick to state that their "average" time to close a loan may be just three weeks, it is certain they also have many loans that take several more weeks to complete. Rest assured, no one really gets paid in the mortgage industry unless a loan closes. Each loan originator, processor, and underwriter are undoubtedly working toward that shared goal.

The underwriter may eventually provide final approval for the loan, known in the industry as a Clear to Close [CTC]. Until this has been granted, there is no guarantee that the loan will be provided. There is also little sense in scheduling a closing on a purchase loan prior to a CTC although many realtors often choose to do so. This only provides an unnecessary expectation for a borrower and seller that the transaction will take place at a predetermined time. Unfortunately, the mortgage approval process is not always as smooth, quick and clean as everyone would hope.

The Closing Disclosure is provided three days prior to the anticipated settlement date. But this may be revised and does not necessarily imply that final approval will be forthcoming.

When a Clear to Close is received, the loan will typically be moved to yet another department at the lender, the Closing Department. This is the moment most have been waiting where the loan is able to be scheduled for closing. However, most closing departments also works on a queue and have only so much daily capacity to meet the demands of a certain number of loan closings. An efficiently run department will have times available the following day at best. When the closer is assigned, they might then, if they have not already done so, cross check the transaction costs with the title company to make sure the numbers on the final Closing Disclosure are correct. Certain other items may need to be addressed at this time, too. For instance, in Texas, every loan at the final stage is subject to a mandatory Texas Attorney review to verify compliance with the Texas Constitution concerning mortgage loans.

At the closing, borrowers will sign in ink and in witness of a notary dozens of documents that include but are not limited to an updated final application, the mortgage, promissory note, deed of trust, and many other boiler-plate, standard documents depending on the investor and loan program.

The title company agent then scans these signed documents and sends them to the lender. Once reviewed and approved for completeness, on a purchase the lender will then wire the appropriate amount to the title company to complete the transaction. On a refinance, the borrower is typically afforded a three day right of rescission to revoke the transaction if they feel compelled to change their mind or need to revise the terms in any manner. These three days include the day of signing, whereby, on the fourth business day, the lender will wire the fund appropriate amount to the title company to be disbursed as agreed.

PART 3: REAL ESTATE PRODUCTIVITY

"That the world after several millennia of steady individual saving, is so poor as it is in accumulated capital-assets, is to be explained, in my opinion, neither by the improvident propensities of mankind, nor even by the destruction of war, but by the high liquidity-premiums formerly attaching to the ownership of land and now attaching to money."

-John Maynard Keyes
THE GENERAL THEORY OF EMPLOYMENT, INTEREST AND MONEY

Make Your Mortgage Matter

29.   Making the Payment

In addition to keeping copies of the three main documents, the mortgage, promissory note, and deed of trust, as well as keeping track of the survey for future use, perhaps the fourth most important document provided at closing is the First Payment Notice. This will be what appears to be three payment stubs or bills showing the amount, due date, and mailing address of where to send each of the first those payments.

The first payment of most all mortgages will be due on the first of the month on the second month following the month of the closing date. Normally, if a loan closes on January 2nd or January 31st, the first payment due date will be March 1. A loan closing on any day in February will typically have a first payment due date of April 1. Mortgage payments in the US are customarily due on the first day of each month, regardless of the day of the month that they close.

And when that payment is made, the interest due and payable is the interest that has accrued from the previous month. Interest accrues in arrears on mortgages. A payment that is made on March 1 will pay February's 30 days of accrued interest based on the outstanding principal balance on February 1. Likewise, the payment due on April 1 will pay 30 days of interest based on the loan balance on March 1.

This standard payment arrangement often leads to some confusion amongst borrowers regarding the interest due at closing when presented with the Closing Disclosure. Consider as an example a purchase loan that will fund on the first day of the month versus the last day of the month. The borrower will be required to pay at closing 30 days of interest for the full loan amount in advance on the first loan. Whereas, a loan funding on the last day of the month will be required to pay just one day of interest. Both loans will have a first payment due date of March 1. Because the lender has no other way to collect January's interest, it must be paid at closing.

Mortgages are commonly, if not always, calculated on a 30/360-day basis in the U.S. As opposed to Treasury and Corporate bonds where the interest is calculated on an actual 365-day basis and each day of ownership of the amount outstanding is accounted for, the mortgage industry is a bit more forgiving, one might say. Where on a mortgage of $500,000 at 6.00% interest, the first day of interest will be:

$500,000 x .06 =$30,000 ÷ 360 = $83.33

Closing on the first of the month as opposed to the last will amount in an additional $83.33 x (30 - 1) = $2,416.67 due at closing. This may make a significant impact on a borrower's ability to source the funds required at closing, the economics of the loan in terms of LTV and/or DTI, or even the financial impact of having that extra ~$2,400 in the bank that may be better used in the future.

Recognize that the decision of when to agree to close and/or fund the loan will likely need to be considered well in advance, like when agreeing on a purchase date in the contract negotiation stage of buying house. With regard to a refinance, it may be determined when the Clear to Close is provided. However, be aware that the CTC is usually only valid for a certain period of time. And delaying the closing may not provide any benefit as the interest due on the previous mortgage included in the payoff for that loan would offset the interest paid in advance on the new loan. Furthermore, delaying the closing on a refinance may result in updated paystubs and other documentation which could jeopardize the approval when holding out for a later date. But if it is a matter of days, it may be worthwhile to consider.

Years ago, borrowers were provided with a payment booklet that had an envelope size sheet or stub for each of the 180 or 360 payments due. Now only three are provided, per law, to make certain borrowers are informed about their first, second and third payment due dates. These will typically if not always show the payment to be made directly to the lender.

All loans in the U.S. are able to be sold. Whether a lender initially intends to retain the servicing as they may disclose or not, their circumstances may change and they always have a right to do so. Indeed, several servicers in the past have been prompted by regulators to sell their mortgage loan servicing portfolios as a result of not so consumer friendly mortgage accounting practices.

Mortgages are often sold and traded in the secondary markets for two different sets of value, the mortgage cash flows and the mortgage servicing rights. The primary value is the mortgage cash flow, the return of principal loan balance on an amortized basis and the majority of its associated monthly interest payment. The mortgage servicing rights are a smaller portion of the monthly interest payment, roughly 0.25% to 0.50% of the interest rate.

Mortgage may initially be sold as either servicing retained or servicing released. If the mortgage is sold with the servicing retained, then the payment will continue to be made to the initial lender. That lender collects the payment and assumes the responsibility of mitigating risk in the event of delinquencies and/or defaults. For that role, they keep that small quarter to half percent of the interest payment and forward the remaining interest and the principal payments to the investor on a timely basis. From time to time, these lenders may elect to sell any number of loans from their portfolio of Mortgage Servicing Rights [MSRs] to another servicing company. There is an active secondary market for these portfolios as their values change based on changing interest rate markets and the potential change in duration of those loans, essentially how long they believe those mortgages may be outstanding and not subject to lower rate refinance transactions, as well as the current credit profile of the underlying loan portfolio.

When the servicing of a mortgage changes hands, the current servicer is required to provide a notice of the sale by mail to the borrower. Likewise, the new servicer is required to make multiple attempts to inform the borrower of where the new payment is to be directed. Borrowers should take heed of these notices. They basically have a grace period of only three months in order to make the appropriate changes to send the payment to the new servicer. This is one reason why the first three payment stubs are provided at the closing. Oftentimes, lenders who are not also in the business of servicing loans will sell the servicing rights prior to even the first payment date of a new loan.

Standard promissory note agreements will convey that the loan will be considered late if the full payment has not been received by the 15th of the month when due on the 1st. Late payments are subject to a late fee, the amount of which may vary from loan to loan and is usually a percentage of the payment amount. Despite a loan being considered late on the 15th, it is not considered delinquent until it is 30 days past due. This is when the lateness may be reported to the credit bureaus with the potential of having a considerable negative impact on a consumer credit score and even impact the ability to finance or refinance real estate in that consumer's future.

According to most promissory notes, when any single payment is 90 days past due the loan will be considered in default and subject to the initiation of foreclosure proceedings. Once a Notice of Default has been filed with the county where the deed of trust had been recorded, the consumer will generally not be able to finance any real estate properties with most lenders until the default has been satisfied in some manner with the servicer who filed the notice.

This has resulted in an unfortunate situation for some borrowers who have sufficient equity in another property. They work under the assumption that they could eventually obtain a cash-out refinance of another property in order to cure a late payment issue with the mortgage on the subject property. However, despite the significant equity position and perceived low risk of lending against that property, they misjudge lenders' willingness to lend to a consumer who is currently facing foreclosure on another property. The lesson of the story is to solve problems sooner rather than later. Most servicing companies really want to help borrowers avoid foreclosure.

Forbearance may be offered if the problem is seen as short term in nature. It should be arranged in advance with the servicing company. For instance, if a surgery would keep the borrower out of work for a temporary period of time, they would be wise to call the servicer prior to a late payment. A forbearance normally allows missed payments to be tacked onto the last payments as if those months of missed payments never existed. This would have little if any negative repercussions on a future ability to borrow.

A modification might be offered which is when certain terms of the promissory note are adjusted to make the new payments more affordable for the borrower's current income situation. This will likely have a negative impact on the borrower's ability to finance real estate in the future. The modification options would be limited to the loss mitigation strategy approved by the investor. The solution offered may not be as accommodative as necessary to provide a reasonable chance for the borrower to afford the new suggested payment.

If the clock is ticking and it is known that a mortgage will eventually become delinquent for reasons unavoidable, there are potential solutions that ought to be explored not ignored. Any options to avoid foreclosure are almost always entirely up to the servicing company. Communicating with them as early as possible when there may be difficulty in making timely payments should always be done without procrastination.

In addition to losing any home equity, time lost should be a major concern. Although lending standards change and also vary between different types of lenders, a foreclosure will generally limit the ability to finance real estate for several years, potentially as many 7 years. Maybe consider renting the house in order to make the payment. Consider selling the house prior to reaching 90 days of delinquencies or a Notice of Default has been recorded. Foreclosure proceedings will eventually result in an eviction by the county sheriff, constable or other office of law enforcement. Deed-in-lieu of foreclosure is no better in the eyes of creditors. This is voluntarily vacating the house rather being forcibly removed. But any adverse action with regard to mortgage real estate is best avoided if at all possible. Missing a payment intentionally is never advisable.

In the same respect, rather than waiting to make a mortgage payment until the 15th of the month, it is beneficial to satisfy the mortgage payment prior to the first of the month. Remember, the interest due the following month is based on the outstanding principal balance on the first of the month. Although the differences may seem as trivial as rounding up the mortgage payment amount to make just a small curtailment, shaving off just a small amount of interest due each month because of an advance payment can amount to a significant interest savings over the life of a loan.

In a similar manner, it is advisable to write in the memo line a note conveying that any additional payment amount be applied only to the principal balance. As stated earlier with regard to servicer not always acting in the best interest of borrowers, servicers have been found to have applied additional payment amounts to the borrower's escrow account rather than to the principal balance as a curtailment, as required by law. Writing a simple note in the memo line may be helpful if additional action is necessary when companies don't act as expected.

Successfully completing all the scheduled payments or paying off the mortgage in advance will result in the servicer providing the borrower a lien release letter. They are also to file the letter with the county. The letter declares that the conditions of the mortgage have been satisfied and the lien holder relinquishes their right to hold a deed of trust on the property. This letter also ought to be kept in duplicate in a safe and another secure place along with survey.

30.   Budget

Money doesn't buy happiness, but lack of money offers sadness. Create a budget for happiness.

"The Consumer Expenditure Surveys (CE) are nationwide household surveys conducted by the U.S. Bureau of Labor Statistics (BLS) to study how U.S. consumers spend their money." (Consumer Expenditures and Income: Overview, 2022) This might be a good place to start from scratch in designing a budget. It may be most useful in providing specific line items for a budget even if not all the lines may be where an individual or family currently spends money. Let those serve as placeholders for the time being. This will create a budget in a way that economists and financial analysts prescribe and allow for that data to be used and analyzed in the same way.

Exhibit 3-1 on the following two pages illustrate the percentage of income spent in various major categories with more specific sub-categories of the typical household budget in 2023. These surveys have barely changed since 1984. And somewhat surprisingly, according to the data the percentage of income spent in each category has also changed very little over the last twenty-five years.

The 2023 survey of 134,556 "consumer units" consisting of 2.5 people in each "unit" or household is consistent with what might be expected from the raw economic data: 1.3 "earners" with a gross income of $101,805; 35% rent versus 38% homeowner with a mortgage and 27% without a mortgage; and, 89% of all households owning or leasing at least one of 1.9 vehicles. Basically, a middle-class married couple with one child or two and two cars.

Exhibit 29-1

U.S. Consumer Expenditure Survey 2023

Income before taxes	100.00%
Income after taxes	86.31%
Savings	10.40%
Average annual expenditures	**75.91%**
Housing	**24.99%**
Shelter	15.22%
Owned dwellings	8.54%
Mortgage interest and charges	3.37%
Property taxes	2.62%
Maintenance, repairs, insurance, and other expenses	2.55%
Rented dwellings	5.27%
Other lodging	1.40%
Utilities, fuels, and public services	4.54%
Natural gas	0.53%
Electricity	1.73%
Fuel oil and other fuels	0.14%
Telephone services	1.38%
Water and other public services	0.77%
Household operations	1.95%
Personal services	0.54%
Other household expenses	1.41%
Housekeeping supplies	0.80%
Laundry and cleaning supplies	0.19%
Other household products	0.51%
Postage and stationery	0.11%
Household furnishings and equipment	2.46%
Household textiles	0.13%
Furniture	0.61%
Floor coverings	0.03%
Major appliances	0.38%
Small appliances and miscellaneous housewares	0.13%
Miscellaneous household equipment	1.19%

Continued on next page...

Exhibit 29-2

U.S. Consumer Expenditure Survey 2023	
Average annual expenditures (Continued)	**75.91%**
Food	**9.81%**
Food at home	5.95%
Food away from home	3.86%
Alcoholic beverages	**0.63%**
Apparel and services	**2.00%**
Transportation	**12.94%**
Vehicle purchases (net outlay)	5.44%
Cars and trucks, new	2.84%
Cars and trucks, used	2.54%
Other vehicles	0.06%
Gasoline and other fuels	2.65%
Other vehicle expenses	3.78%
Vehicle finance charges	0.35%
Maintenance and repairs	0.96%
Vehicle rental, leases, licenses, and other charges	0.72%
Vehicle insurance	1.74%
Public and other transportation	1.08%
Healthcare	**6.05%**
Health insurance	3.98%
Medical services	1.23%
Drugs	0.58%
Medical supplies	0.26%
Entertainment	**3.57%**
Personal care products and services	**0.93%**
Reading	**0.11%**
Education	**1.63%**
Tobacco products and smoking supplies	**0.36%**
Miscellaneous	**1.16%**
Cash contributions	**2.34%**
Personal insurance and pensions	**9.39%**
Life and other personal insurance	0.54%
Pensions and Social Security	8.85%

(Consumer Expenditures and Income: Overview, 2022)

A closer inspection of these percentages suggest they may not be a good basis to start a real budget. Again, the line items are valid, but the percentages do not tell the right story most glaringly for the cost of shelter.

Housing is the largest expenditure at nearly 25% of the average US consumer budget. "Shelter", however, only constitutes 15.22% of the overall budget. While the other roughly 10% is reportedly spent on utilities, cleaning, and home goods.

This 15.22% for shelter is largely the same as the payment-to-income ratio, or PTI, as discussed in Chapter 16. The debt-to-income ratio, DTI, includes other debt payments. According to the survey, the only line items that would be recognized is the net outlay for vehicles of 5.44%. Combining the two implies that the average consumer's DTI is a mere 20.66%.

It should be recognized that 27% of households own their house without a mortgage, per the CE. This is a clear reason why the 20.66% equivalent DTI may be misleading. And while another 25% rent, the 20.66% equivalent DTI, or more importantly the 15.22% PTI, must be adjusted further by anyone looking to use the data as a starting point for their budget.

What is remarkable is that the CE rationalizes that only about 15% of consumer expenditures are allocated to shelter. Yet, the maximum allowable to be spent on shelter when seeking approval for a government or quasi-government (FNMA or FHLMC) loan is 50%. The CE's average 20.66% equivalent DTI versus the increasing standard and/or limit over the last thirty years from 36% to 43% to 50% shows how consumers who decide to finance at those upper levels of their gross income must be stretching the remainder of their budget extraordinarily thin.

Much caution should be granted when increasing the budget line item of shelter from 15% toward those upper limits. It is questionable that many households spend as little as 15% on the cost of shelter in most cities throughout the United States.

Breaking down the numbers, on $101,805 income spending 2.62% on property taxes amounts to $2,666 annually. In Texas, property taxes are approximately 2% of the house value. This implies a home value of $133,300 or roughly 1/3rd the average home price in Texas.

Digging deeper, if this theoretical $133,300 home were purchased with a mortgage of 80% of the loan value with a 6% mortgage interest rate, the monthly principal & interest payment would be $636.18. That is $7,634.16 annually or 7.50% of the $101,805 gross income. This is nearly twice the percentage of the cost indicated by the survey. That math may be realistic when the survey suggests 27% of homeowner respondents do not have a mortgage.

Now consider that in December of 2023, the same year as the CE, the median home sales price in Texas was $332,300. (Roberson & McMeans, 2024) With an 80% LTV and an average mortgage rate that month of about 6.75% (30 Year Fixed Rate Mortgages, 2025), that annual principal, interest, taxes, and insurance payment [PITI] would have totaled $31,508.08. This is 30.95% of the average income and likely way more in line with front-end or PTI ratios that is witnessed in the mortgage industry of late. That 30% is twice the cost of shelter as recognized by the CE survey.

The point is that if the budgeted percentage for the mortgage payment, property taxes and homeowners insurance is higher because the price of the house is higher, then other line items in the budget must be reduced substantially or eliminated in order to make up the difference.

Without recognizing and accounting for this fact, or worse yet not even truly having a budget to abide by, will lead to significant hardship very quickly when purchasing. Payment shock is the appropriate mortgage industry term. Some underwriting protocols evaluate the difference of a current rental payment versus the proposed PITI payment of first-time home buyers. Limitations often range from 250% to 350%.

In the most recent example, the new monthly payment would be $2,625.67. As a guide, that borrower would need to document rental payments of at least $1,000 for the previous year under certain mortgage programs. If taken one step further, this borrower should have been able to at least save the difference in rent versus the new payment over the course of the previous year, about $20,000. With a 20% down payment and about $10,000 in closing costs, or about $75,000, this could be easily established.

Had this same borrower only been able to provide 5% down payment along with the closing costs they would still have needed to save about $2,000 each month over the course of the previous year. But the impact of the payment in financing 95% versus 80% would be an increase in payment of approximately $400 per month. Then, the previous rent amount would have needed to be nearer $1,250 to be within a 250% payment shock metric.

Much more importantly, the PITI would now be near 37%. Financing may be obtainable yet not affordable. Remember, housing affordability is best to be thought of as being able to comfortably make the monthly payments to keep that shelter.

31.   Asset/Liability Management

Asset/Liability Management is an essential element in the way banks and many other institutions maintain their financial solvency. They use this financial planning and analysis to increase stability while at the same time reducing the risk of becoming illiquid.

Banks get "demand deposits" of cash from payroll deposits and other customer sources of income. But they never know exactly when depositors will withdraw that money. People pay bills and buy things every day so banks must keep some money on hand to meet those needs.

Banks are in business to lend their excess deposits. Their profit is largely generated from their Net Interest Margin [NIM]. This is the difference between the interest income they earn on lending money or investing in assets versus the interest expense that they pay customers, if any, for holding money in their checking, savings, money market, or any other cost of funds, like the money banks might borrow from other commercial banks or even the Federal Reserve.

Just like on any Balance Sheet, bank assets are their cash, the loans they make, and other investments they own. On their Income Statement, these assets translate into interest income. Their liabilities on the Balance Sheet are mainly the demand deposits, essentially money they have borrowed and owe to their checking and savings customers. That cost of borrowed money is the interest expense on the Income Statement.

The primary concern of a bank is to make sure that they have ample cash available every day. They simply can't run out of money. As long as the loan payments, or cash inflows, they receive from their assets are similar or less than the deposit withdrawals, the cash outflows, they should be able to maintain enough cash to survive another day. This is understood by looking at their Cash Flow Statement.

For an individual, the same applies. Their income must be greater than their expenses. Certainly at least one component of financial stability is dependent on creating a budget and having the discipline to spend within those limitations set by the budget. This is truly the number one concern of financial responsibility, financial freedom, and the way to best understand and define wealth.

An honest examination of assets and liabilities, income and expenses is essential to financial stability. Questions to consider may include how much to save independently versus how much to put in a 401(k). How does a consumer plan for life events like marriage and children are all better to have ironed out at the earliest stages of life. The type of career chosen or role in life should be of great contemplation, too. Are those expected earnings cyclical because of the industry or nature of the work. Will the income be commission based, hourly or salaried, and how might that effect the ability to manage cash flows.

These are all important considerations and interdependent. Having a holistic view of cash-flow regularity while at the same time understanding regular and irregular expenses is at the heart of ALM management. Hardship or success will be determined by how well fluctuations in cash flow are managed.

And this is well beyond the scope of most loan originators and scarcely thought through in any lending guidelines.

The key driver of a good Asset/Liability Management strategy is in understanding the amount of cash that will be needed today, tomorrow, and in the future. Only when that is recognized can it be determined if asset alternatives to cash are prudent.

In a simplistic consumer model, there are likely at least three assets: cash, a house and a car. And then there are hopefully only two liabilities: a mortgage and an auto loan. On the Cash Flow Statement, the amount of cash available must meet the periodic demands of the mortgage payment and the auto loan payment. Income from a job adds to the cash position. When that income is greater than the debt payments and other expenses, obviously, the cash position grows.

As the cash position grows larger, investing it in another asset that produces additional income without risk to meeting future payment obligations is the tricky part.

CDs are offered from banks as an investment with a penalty if the money is converted back to cash prior to the maturity date. A 3-month or a 6-month CD would incur a penalty if redeemed before three or six months, respectively. For that penalty risk, the reward is an interest rate higher than what would be provided if the money sat in that bank's checking or savings account, presumably.

Imagine enough cash savings to cover six months of debt payments and expenses. Perhaps 1/6th of that amount could be invested in a 6-month Certificate of Deposit. And each month, another 1/6th could be invested in another 6-month CD. As one CD matures every month, that cash becomes available to pay the bills if current income has faltered.

A strategy like this is a conservative approach because it doesn't risk the immediate need for all of the cash but rather matches the future availability with the future potential need for it. The simple technique is called laddering. It is used by banks. In fact, banks offer CDs simply because they believe they can safely lend or invest that money over the same period at a higher rate. They invest the CD proceeds in something riskier to create a positive net interest margin.

Converting a primary residence to a rental property can be just as efficient. When the potential rent is higher or the same as the mortgage payment and expenses, then the cash flow is matched.

Seller financing offers a similar benefit. Receiving a monthly mortgage principal & interest payment provides cash flow akin to a rental income stream by replacing a property management company with a mortgage loan servicer. If a house is sold in the traditional manner for the cash proceeds, those monies are still likely to be re-invested in an asset that provides future cash flows.

Financial stability is obtainable only by securing future income to cover future expenses. Financial freedom does not require being free of debt. Debt ought to be used to finance assets that produce timely income greater than the timely payments required by that debt along with any expenses related to that asset.

32.   Interest Rate Cycles

Mortgage interest rates are tied to the US Ten Year Treasury. Most mortgages are sold upstream to Wall Street Primary Dealers who use them as collateral to issue MBS guaranteed by FNMA or FHLMC. These are offered to investors who receive a share of the monthly principal & interest payment proportional to their investment. This is referred to as a "pass-through" security.

Alternatively, the mortgages are used as collateral for Real Estate Mortgage Investment Conduits [REMICs], a program also guaranteed by FNMA or FHLMC]. These CMOs are derivatives where the monthly principal & interest cash flows are distributed to different bond classes according to singular or various pre-determined rules. Institutional investors use these mortgage derivatives to better control when they receive the return of their principal investment so they are more accurately matched with their future need for that cash.

As an example, a life insurance company may want to invest all of the premiums they receive from policy owners under age 40 and not want to see any return of that bucket of cash for 20 years. Accordingly, a tranche of a CMO can be structured to meet or try to meet those specifications, called a Z bond.

Once a mortgage promissory note is signed by a borrower, the lender has the ability to sell that note. These are bought until at least a large enough pool of mortgages is amassed to efficiently create an MBS or CMO. The total principal amount of that pool will be hedged against Ten Year Treasurys. For instance, if $1 billion of mortgages are purchased by a primary dealer, they might choose to sell $1 billion of Ten Year Treasurys in order to fund the purchase. As they sell the ensuing MBS or CMO to investors, they buy back an equal amount of Ten Year Treasurys. By doing so, they utilize very little of their own capital.

The duration, or average time of receipt of payments, of a 30-year mortgage pass-through security is more approximate to 10 years, not 30. The amortization schedule, curtailments and total repayment option afforded to the borrower reduces the normal duration. Thus, because the Ten Year Treasury is used to offset or hedge the position, changes in yield to the Ten Year Treasury have a direct correlation to the change in mortgage interest rates.

Additionally, the Mortgage Basis Spread is the difference between Ten Year Treasurys and mortgage interest rates. This difference in higher yield is produced by the investor demanding a higher return because of the additional risk assumed by investing in US mortgages versus the lesser risk of US Treasurys. Numerous factors influence each investors assessment of this risk.

Prepayment risk is the primary factor. The borrower has a right to repay any or all of the borrowed amount at any time. The brains that develop mortgage prepayment models for Wall Street are former nuclear submarine engineers and rocket scientists, literally from the Navy and NASA. The problem they analyze is that typically when prepayments increase or decrease is exactly when investors don't want those cash flows. For instance, if a current mortgage rate is 8% but can be refinanced at 5%, the borrower probably will. The investor bought an 8% coupon for a presupposed period of time and was counting on the cash flow over that time frame to provide an implied rate of return. But now they get their cash back and can only re-invest it at 5% all else being equal, offering a lower rate of return over the same period.

Or, if mortgage rates go from 4% to 7%, the investor might have initially thought the duration would be a normal 10 years. But with a contraction in curtailments and full repayments because of a smart unwillingness by the borrower to exchange that mortgage for another house financed at a higher rate, the perceived average duration extends out to 12 or 15 years. That investor is missing out on the cash flow that they would otherwise be able to reinvest in the meantime at higher market rates.

For these reasons and others, mortgage interest rates run parallel to Ten Year Treasurys. Over the last 20 years, that spread has averaged 185 basis points and a majority of the time is range bound between 1.50 and 2.00%. It is worthwhile for the consumer to understand these market features because they may be able to better take advantage of interest rate cycles.

Exhibit 31-1

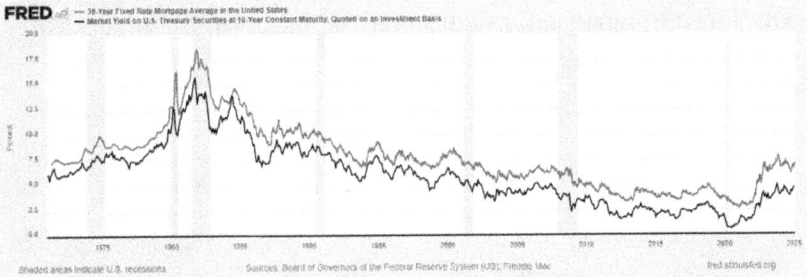

(Freddie Mac, 2025) (Board of Governors of the Federal Reserve System (US), 2025)

If it appears the Ten Year Treasury is trending higher or near the top of a cyclical pattern and the mortgage basis spread is wider than normal, there would likely be a greater probability that in the future, near or far, market rates will fall and the mortgage basis spread will tighten presenting an opportunity to refinance. Taking advantage of a lender credit or something closer to a no-cost loan when purchasing a home would be more advisable in this type of scenario. Even though that current rate would be higher, the expectation is that it would only be for a temporary or short-term basis.

Another way to attempt to take of advantage of higher rates is to consider an ARM. An ARM might achieve the same effect of paying a lower interest in the future without the need or cost, if any, to refinance. But there may be a reason to refinance, such as removing mortgage insurance. On a loan with mortgage insurance, an ARM may not be the best option.

The opposite would be true if or when mortgage rates were low, rather, when they are so low that the rate presented would be acceptable for long term financing. Then consideration to buy down the rate to the lowest possible rate offered may be worthwhile only so long as there is also an expectation to own that house for a long time.

These types of interest rate bias bets and all other mortgage strategies should be discussed thoroughly with a licensed and experienced mortgage professional who more than adequately understands the concepts at play.

33.   Leverage

Over the course of a lifetime, most adults who are fortunate enough to have initially become a first-time home buyer will eventually have owned and subsequently sold five or six houses. The story begins with a young newlywed couple buying a "starter" home with every intention of living there for the rest of their lives. They are encouraged to believe they must at least live there for thirty years because they have committed to a thirty-year mortgage.

But after several years, a few offspring, and a promotion they set their sights on a slightly larger home in a slightly better school district. They sell their first home, take the equity appreciation and plunk it all down on that next house. Rinse and repeat about five years later.

Around the age of 45 and amidst their peak earning years they are sold on new construction with a pool and more garage space, maybe a media room. Once again, they sell their current house to use that equity for the down payment.

Ten years later, the kids have moved out and the pool is seldom used and it is time to downsize or "right size" into their fifth home.

There is no fault in this happily married couple's desire to improve their accommodations to suit the needs of their family. The mistake made, however, is in selling each of their previous houses to seize the equity for the down payment on the next house.

Planning and budgeting for this quite common trajectory is the recommendation. What ought to be encouraged is to deliberately budget to build enough in a savings or investment account to have the liquidity for a down payment on the next house, and then the next house, and then the next. This is the way to build wealth.

Recall the application of the Debt Service Coverage Ratio. When a home is financed prudently, the potential rental income is sufficient to pay the mortgage principal & interest, property taxes, homeowners insurance and home owner association dues, if any.

Therefore, the renter is paying off the mortgage. Leverage by way of a mortgage in real estate is most advantageous because of the rental income available to pay back that leverage. When a consumer sells their current house and uses the proceeds to purchase their next home, it is their income only that is used to pay back the mortgage. And they lose the opportunity for future income.

Certain institutional investors, like hedge funds, use leverage to multiply their returns on an investment. A conservative hedge fund might apply 20x leverage by borrowing money at, as an example, a 4% interest rate. If they purchase an investment that yields 6%, with only their initial $1, they earn $0.06 annually. If they borrower $19 at 4%, the financed leverage would cost $0.76 per year. And now with $20 invested at 6%, they would earn $1.20 - $0.76 = $0.44 with the same initial dollar but applying leverage.

This example could also be abundantly risky because if the $20 loses only 5%, their $1 of equity is wiped out. If their financing is subject to a margin call, they may be forced to sell the $19 of remaining value to repay the loan. But mortgages are not subject to a forced liquidation because of a decrease in value.

Financing a house is perhaps the only way individuals or households can purchase an appreciating asset using leverage. The only other similar in function comparison that comes to mind would be an employer matching contribution in a retirement account. If an employee puts in a $1, the employer puts in a $1 which still might be subject to some vesting period. This dollar-for-dollar match would be akin to 2x leverage. With a house purchased using a mortgage with an 80% LTV, the borrower puts in a dollar and the lender puts in $4, for 5x leverage. With a 90% LTV, the borrower puts in a $1 and the lender puts in $9, for 10x leverage.

If a house is financed at 6% with a 30-year level pay, fixed rate mortgage, the monthly principal & interest payment is $600 per $100,000 financed ($599.55 to be exact). With a 90% LTV, $11,111.11 is required to buy a $111,111.11 house. When the mortgage is paid off, yes, in 30 years, that $11,111.11 initial investment would presumably still generate at least $600 per month in cash flow if bought with a favorable DSCR.

In comparison, an investment of $120,000 earning 6% would be needed to earn the same $7,200 year in income. However, that same $11,111.11 invested today in another asset would need to earn 8.25% compounded annually every year for 30 years to reach $120,000. Alternatively, investing $11,111.11 at 7.468% compounded annually every year would amass $94,611.35. This amount again earning nearly 7.50% in year 31 would generate $7,200. That would be an impressive track record for any money manager.

Arguably the most efficient way for an individual to acquire future cash flows is to leverage their cash with a level pay, fixed rate mortgage. Those 360 monthly principal and interest payments remain the same while the future stream of rental payments will tend to consistently out-pace or run even with inflation. As the shelter components of property taxes, homeowners insurance and maintenance costs increase due to inflation, so too does the rental value to cover those expenses.

When presented with the idea of owning a rental property most people quip that they don't want to be a landlord. The good news is that separation can easily be created to maintain real estate investments with a hands-off approach. Not all property management companies are created equally. It is important to spend a minute to find one that is managed well and provides the services required. This could include finding good tenants and evicting bad tenants when necessary. It would likely include collecting the monthly rental payment and forwarding those funds to you. It most definitely should include taking the midnight phone call to sort a plumbing issue along with any routine maintenance and repairs.

In the eyes of a distant investor, they would never want to have any direct contact with the tenants or need to ever step foot on the property. The property manager fills the roles of the "landlord" for a fee in the range of one month's rent per year plus any expenses incurred in the maintenance of the property.

When purchasing a house for a primary residence, it is appropriate to consider the immediate usefulness of it as a family home but also for future use as an investment property. Rather than ever selling a house, it is most advantageous to retain it for the potential of its future positive cash flows. This requires saving enough money for the down payment on the next house.

While there may be no inclination or need to accumulate dozens of rental properties, most people will own and live in several houses throughout their life. If they budget enough savings for the down payment of each next primary residence home purchase, they are able to once again take advantage of the opportunity to leverage their money. At the same time, this affords them the opportunity to convert their current primary residence into an income generating investment property. That opportunity ought to be exercised.

34.   Wealth Creation

As was once explained perfectly by a Wall Street genius, wealth is best viewed as a lake of money.

Earned income, a paycheck, is only a river. That water in the river naturally flows away downstream in the form of living expenses.

A dam must be built to limit these expenses in order to create a lake.

True wealth is when the lake is large enough to never dry up for the remainder of one's life despite the constant flow of water out of the dam.

Earned income is not wealth because it is not wholly reliable. A person can lose their job, their industry may collapse, they might get injured and no longer be able to work, and eventually they will be forced to retire if they don't first die. The river might run dry.

The key to making that lake big enough to achieve true wealth is largely dependent on two things. The first and most important is to build a good, strong dam as early in life as possible.

Financial problems occur most commonly because people live above their means. Many people spend more money than they make probably expecting to eventually make more and cover the difference later. But as they make more, they spend more. Maybe they do not have the proper limitations on spending, enough discipline, or maybe not even a budget. For whatever reason, they aren't saving enough for the future.

The advisable course of action is to limit the growth of expenses regardless of incremental increases in earned income. It is the frugal, millionaire next door tactic. (Stanley, 2010) This is the dam that creates excess and abundant savings over time.

How that savings is invested is the second key to turn a puddle into a pond and grow it into a lake of money. It is simply not enough to put it in a savings account earning nearly zero percent. Inflation is an uncontrollable increase in future expenses. At the very least, that money must earn more than the annual rate of inflation.

Residential real estate financing provides consumers the required fundamental advantages necessary to grow wealth. These are the same principles that institutional investors use to their advantage when investing in real estate. Understand, though, this is not a get rich quick scheme. The concepts are why the most conservative financial institutions seek Residential and Commercial Mortgage-Backed Securities as their first choice when investing capital that they dare not lose. These are also often the core investments in many intermediate- and long-term bond funds.

The simple strategy covers a lifetime of diligent home financing based on the lake effect. It is about generating increased cash flows over time, passive income that continues to fill the lake. Where once it was predominantly thought that "cash is king" in investment circles, "cash flow is king" is the assertion here. Cash flow provides an ability to pay expenses. Excess cash flow provides additional savings to invest in more cash flow generating assets. These types of investments could just as well be dividend paying stocks, bonds, Real Estate Investment Trusts [REITS], or annuities. But none of those assets can be purchased with leverage.

35.   Conclusion

The price of a house is an arbitrary value. Home price appreciation is a product of inflation. And inflation is produced solely by increasing the money supply, or printing money. The only time that the market price of a house is of concern is if it is being bought, refinanced, or sold.

The greatest advantage presented with residential real estate is that it has nearly everlasting utility value. Built in 1148, Saltford Manor House "is thought to be the oldest continuously occupied private house in England." (Saltford Manor House, 2025) When a house is properly maintained then it might last for generations. Imagine accumulating 850 years of cash flow if that house had been rented out over all those years. Real estate rarely, if ever, ought to be sold.

When never sold, a house becomes the children's house and a house for future generations of children and their families. Maybe those children live in the house. Maybe they rent it out and the positive cash flow from the property helps defray the cost of their chosen shelter or other living expenses. Yes, there are always property taxes, insurance and maintenance. It may even be best at some point to tear it down and build a new house or something else on the land. But the value of the land has been bought and paid for.

Houses ought to be purchased and financed within reasonable measures of affordability. Consider a PTI and DTI less than 30%, a DSCR above 1% where the potential current rental income is greater than the PITI, and with a standing budget for savings large enough for a downpayment on another house within five or ten years. With these constraints in place, financial stability is vastly improved.

Contrarily, obtaining a mortgage with a payment that puts a consumer's DTI nearer the maximum allowable of 50% greatly discourages financial stability. That consumer enters into a precarious situation when any unforeseen or emergency expenses arise and very little consideration for savings. Their ability to readily and consistently meet future debt payment obligations is treacherous.

The ability to obtain multiple assets using leverage not available with other investments is why residential real estate ought to be considered as the best asset class for consumers. People think of their home as their largest investment and the financing should be aligned with a buy and hold investment strategy. Future rental income may continue to pay the mortgage, reducing that leverage. A 30-year level pay, fixed rate mortgage payment stays the same or may even be refinanced lower, but will eventually be zero when the loan is paid off. At the same time, rent tends to increase in tandem and often in excess of inflation. This compensates for the rising cost of future expenses due to inflation.

So, too, the present value of that initial mortgage payment ought to be somewhat equivalent to its present purchasing power. In other words, future passive rental net income ought to be considered a very reliable source of income for retirement planning.

APPENDIX A

Uniform Appraisal Dataset Definitions

Condition Ratings and Definitions

C1

The improvements have been recently constructed and have not been previously occupied. The entire structure and all components are new and the dwelling features no physical depreciation.

Note: *Newly constructed improvements that feature recycled or previously used materials and/or components can be considered new dwellings provided that the dwelling is placed on a 100 percent new foundation and the recycled materials and the recycled components have been rehabilitated/remanufactured into like-new condition. Improvements that have not been previously occupied are not considered "new" if they have any significant physical depreciation (that is, newly constructed dwellings that have been vacant for an extended period of time without adequate maintenance or upkeep).*

C2

The improvements feature no deferred maintenance, little or no physical depreciation, and require no repairs. Virtually all building components are new or have been recently repaired, refinished, or rehabilitated. All outdated components and finishes have been updated and/or replaced with components that meet current standards. Dwellings in this category are either almost new or have been recently completely renovated and are similar in condition to new construction.

Note: *The improvements represent a relatively new property that is well maintained with no deferred maintenance and little or no physical depreciation, or an older property that has been recently completely renovated.*

C3

The improvements are well maintained and feature limited physical depreciation due to
normal wear and tear. Some components, but not every major building component, may be updated or recently rehabilitated. The structure has been well maintained.

Note: *The improvement is in its first cycle of replacing short-lived building components (appliances, floor coverings, HVAC, etc.) and is being well maintained. Its estimated effective age is less than its actual age. It also may reflect a property in which the majority of short-lived building components have been replaced but not to the level of a complete renovation.*

C4

The improvements feature some minor deferred maintenance and physical deterioration due to normal wear and tear. The dwelling has been adequately maintained and requires only minimal repairs to building components/mechanical systems and cosmetic repairs. All major building components have been adequately maintained and are functionally adequate.

Note: *The estimated effective age may be close to or equal to its actual age. It reflects a property in which some of the short-lived building components have been replaced, and some short-lived building components are at or near the end of their physical life expectancy; however, they still function adequately. Most minor repairs have been addressed on an ongoing basis resulting in an adequately maintained property.*

C5

The improvements feature obvious deferred maintenance and are in need of some
significant repairs. Some building components need repairs, rehabilitation, or updating. The functional utility and overall livability are somewhat diminished due to condition, but the dwelling remains useable and functional as a residence.

Note: *Some significant repairs are needed to the improvements due to the lack of adequate maintenance. It reflects a property in which many of its short-lived building components are at the end of or have exceeded their physical life expectancy but remain functional.*

C6

The improvements have substantial damage or deferred maintenance with deficiencies or defects that are severe enough to affect the safety, soundness, or structural integrity of the improvements. The improvements are in need of substantial repairs and rehabilitation, including many or most major components.

Note: *Substantial repairs are needed to the improvements due to the lack of adequate maintenance or property damage. It reflects a property with conditions severe enough to affect the safety, soundness, or structural integrity of the improvements.*

Quality Ratings and Definitions

Q1

Dwellings with this quality rating are usually unique structures that are individually designed by an architect for a specified user. Such residences typically are constructed from detailed architectural plans and specifications and feature an exceptionally high level of workmanship and exceptionally high-grade materials throughout the interior and exterior of the structure. The design features exceptionally high-quality exterior refinements and ornamentation, and exceptionally high-quality interior refinements. The workmanship, materials, and finishes throughout the dwelling are of exceptionally high quality.

Q2

Dwellings with this quality rating are often custom designed for construction on an individual property owner's site. However, dwellings in this quality grade are also found in high-quality tract developments featuring residences constructed from individual plans or from highly modified or upgraded plans. The design features detailed, high- quality exterior ornamentation, high-quality interior refinements, and detail. The workmanship, materials, and finishes throughout the dwelling are generally of high or very high quality.

Q3

Dwellings with this quality rating are residences of higher quality built from individual or readily available designer plans in above-standard residential tract developments or on an individual property owner's site. The design includes significant exterior ornamentation and interiors that are well finished. The workmanship exceeds acceptable standards and many materials and finishes throughout the dwelling have been upgraded from "stock" standards.

Q4

Dwellings with this quality rating meet or exceed the requirements of applicable building codes. Standard or modified standard building plans are utilized and the design includes adequate fenestration and some exterior ornamentation and interior refinements. Materials, workmanship, finish, and equipment are of stock or builder grade and may feature some upgrades.

Q5

Dwellings with this quality rating feature economy of construction and basic functionality as main considerations. Such dwellings feature a plain design using readily available or basic floor plans featuring minimal fenestration and basic finishes with minimal exterior ornamentation and limited interior detail. These dwellings meet minimum building codes and are constructed with inexpensive, stock materials with limited refinements and upgrades.

Q6

Dwellings with this quality rating are of basic quality and lower cost; some may not be suitable for year-round occupancy. Such dwellings are often built with simple plans or without plans, often utilizing the lowest quality building materials. Such dwellings are often built or expanded by persons who are professionally unskilled or possess only minimal construction skills. Electrical, plumbing, and other mechanical systems and equipment may be minimal or non-existent. Older dwellings may feature one or more substandard or non-conforming additions to the original structure.

Definitions of Not Updated, Updated, and Remodeled
Not Updated
Little or no updating or modernization. This description includes, but is not limited to, new homes.

Residential properties of fifteen years of age or less often reflect an original condition with no updating if no major components have been replaced or updated. Those over fifteen years of age are also considered not updated if the appliances, fixtures, and finishes are predominantly dated. An area that is 'Not Updated' may still be well maintained and fully functional, and this rating does not necessarily imply deferred maintenance or physical/functional deterioration.

Updated
The area of the home has been modified to meet current market expectations. These modifications are limited in terms of both scope and cost.

An updated area of the home should have an improved look and feel, or functional utility. Changes that constitute updates include refurbishment and/or replacing components to meet existing market expectations. Updates do not include significant alterations to the existing structure.

Remodeled
Significant finish and/or structural changes have been made that increase utility and appeal through complete replacement and/or expansion.

A remodeled area reflects fundamental changes that include multiple alterations. These alterations may include some or all of the following: replacement of a major component (cabinet(s), bathtub, or bathroom tile), relocation of plumbing/gas fixtures/appliances, significant structural alterations (relocating walls, and/or the addition of square footage). This would include a complete gutting and rebuild.

APPENDIX B

Uniform Residential Loan Application [URLA], Page 1

To be completed by the Lender:
Lender Loan No./Universal Loan Identifier _____ Agency Case No. _____

Uniform Residential Loan Application

Verify and complete the information on this application. If you are applying for this loan with others, each additional Borrower must provide information as directed by your Lender.

Section 1: Borrower Information. This section asks about your personal information and your income from employment and other sources, such as retirement, that you want considered to qualify for this loan.

1a. Personal Information

Name (First, Middle, Last, Suffix)

Alternate Names – List any names by which you are known or any names under which credit was previously received (First, Middle, Last, Suffix)

Social Security Number ___ - ___ - ___
(or Individual Taxpayer Identification Number)

Date of Birth
(mm/dd/yyyy)
___ / ___ / ___

Citizenship
○ U.S. Citizen
○ Permanent Resident Alien
○ Non-Permanent Resident Alien

Type of Credit
○ I am applying for **individual credit.**
○ I am applying for **joint credit.** Total Number of Borrowers: ___
Each Borrower intends to apply for joint credit. **Your initials:** ___

List Name(s) of Other Borrower(s) Applying for this Loan
(First, Middle, Last, Suffix) – Use a separator between names

Marital Status
○ Married
○ Separated
○ Unmarried
(Single, Divorced, Widowed, Civil Union, Domestic Partnership, Registered Reciprocal Beneficiary Relationship)

Dependents (not listed by another Borrower)
Number ___
Ages ___

Contact Information
Home Phone (___) ___ - ___
Cell Phone (___) ___ - ___
Work Phone (___) ___ - ___ Ext. ___
Email ___

Current Address
Street ___ Unit # ___
City ___ State ___ ZIP ___ Country ___
How Long at Current Address? ___ Years ___ Months **Housing** ○ No primary housing expense ○ Own ○ Rent ($ ___ /month)

If at Current Address for LESS than 2 years, list Former Address ☐ Does not apply
Street ___ Unit # ___
City ___ State ___ ZIP ___ Country ___
How Long at Former Address? ___ Years ___ Months **Housing** ○ No primary housing expense ○ Own ○ Rent ($ ___ /month)

Mailing Address – if different from Current Address ☐ Does not apply
Street ___ Unit # ___
City ___ State ___ ZIP ___ Country ___

1b. Current Employment/Self-Employment and Income ☐ Does not apply

Employer or Business Name ___ Phone (___) ___ - ___
Street ___ Unit # ___
City ___ State ___ ZIP ___ Country ___

Position or Title ___
Start Date ___ / ___ / ___ (mm/dd/yyyy)
How long in this line of work? ___ Years ___ Months

Check if this statement applies:
☐ I am employed by a family member, property seller, real estate agent, or other party to the transaction.

☐ **Check if you are the Business Owner or Self-Employed**
○ I have an ownership share of less than 25%. **Monthly Income (or Loss)**
○ I have an ownership share of 25% or more. $ ___

Gross Monthly Income
Base	$ ___	/month
Overtime	$ ___	/month
Bonus	$ ___	/month
Commission	$ ___	/month
Military Entitlements	$ ___	/month
Other	$ ___	/month
TOTAL	$ ___	**0.00**/month

Uniform Residential Loan Application
Freddie Mac Form 65 · Fannie Mae Form 1003
Effective 1/2021

Uniform Residential Loan Application [URLA], Page 2

1c. IF APPLICABLE, Complete Information for Additional Employment/Self-Employment and Income ☐ *Does not apply*

Employer or Business Name	Phone ( ) –	Gross Monthly Income		
Street	Unit #	Base	$	/month
City State ZIP Country		Overtime	$	/month
		Bonus	$	/month

Position or Title	Check if this statement applies:	Commission	$	/month
Start Date / / (mm/dd/yyyy)	☐ I am employed by a family member, property seller, real estate agent, or other party to the transaction.	Military Entitlements	$	/month
How long in this line of work? ___ Years ___ Months		Other	$	/month

☐ Check if you are the Business Owner or Self-Employed   ◯ I have an ownership share of less than 25%.   **Monthly Income (or Loss)**   ◯ I have an ownership share of 25% or more. $ _____

TOTAL $ _____ 0.00/month

1d. IF APPLICABLE, Complete Information for Previous Employment/Self-Employment and Income ☐ *Does not apply*

Provide at least 2 years of current and previous employment and income.

Employer or Business Name		Previous Gross Monthly
Street Unit #		Income $ _____ /month
City State ZIP Country		

Position or Title	
Start Date / / (mm/dd/yyyy)	☐ Check if you were the Business Owner or Self-Employed
End Date / / (mm/dd/yyyy)	

1e. Income from Other Sources ☐ *Does not apply*

Include income from other sources below. Under Income Source, choose from the sources listed here:

- Alimony
- Automobile Allowance
- Boarder Income
- Capital Gains
- Child Support
- Disability
- Foster Care
- Housing or Parsonage
- Interest and Dividends
- Mortgage Credit Certificate
- Mortgage Differential Payments
- Notes Receivable
- Public Assistance
- Retirement (e.g. Pension, IRA)
- Royalty Payments
- Separate Maintenance
- Social Security
- Trust
- Unemployment Benefits
- VA Compensation
- Other

NOTE: *Reveal alimony, child support, separate maintenance, or other income ONLY IF you want it considered in determining your qualification for this loan.*

Income Source – use list above	Monthly Income
	$
	$
	$
Provide TOTAL Amount Here	$ 0.00

Borrower Name: _____
Uniform Residential Loan Application
Freddie Mac Form 65 · Fannie Mae Form 1003
Effective 1/2021

Uniform Residential Loan Application [URLA], Page 3

Section 2: Financial Information — Assets and Liabilities. This section asks about things you own that are worth money and that you want considered to qualify for this loan. It then asks about your liabilities (or debts) that you pay each month, such as credit cards, alimony, or other expenses.

2a. Assets -- Bank Accounts, Retirement, and Other Accounts You Have

Include all accounts below. Under Account Type, choose from the types listed here:
- Checking
- Savings
- Money Market
- Certificate of Deposit
- Mutual Fund
- Stocks
- Stock Options
- Bonds
- Retirement (e.g., 401k, IRA)
- Bridge Loan Proceeds
- Individual Development Account
- Trust Account
- Cash Value of Life Insurance (used for the transaction)

Account Type – use list above	Financial Institution	Account Number	Cash or Market Value
			$
			$
			$
			$
			$
		Provide TOTAL Amount Here	$ 0.00

2b. Other Assets and Credits You Have   ☐ Does not apply

Include all other assets and credits below. Under Asset or Credit Type, choose from the types listed here:

Assets
- Proceeds from Real Estate Property to be sold on or before closing
- Proceeds from Sale of Non-Real Estate Asset
- Secured Borrowed Funds
- Unsecured Borrowed Funds
- Other

Credits
- Earnest Money
- Employer Assistance
- Lot Equity
- Relocation Funds
- Rent Credit
- Sweat Equity
- Trade Equity

Asset or Credit Type – use list above	Cash or Market Value
	$
	$
	$
	$
Provide TOTAL Amount Here	$ 0.00

2c. Liabilities -- Credit Cards, Other Debts, and Leases that You Owe   ☐ Does not apply

List all liabilities below (except real estate) and include deferred payments. Under Account Type, choose from the types listed here:
- Revolving (e.g., credit cards)
- Installment (e.g., car, student, personal loans)
- Open 30-Day (balance paid monthly)
- Lease (not real estate)
- Other

Account Type – use list above	Company Name	Account Number	Unpaid Balance	To be paid off at or before closing	Monthly Payment
			$	☐	$
			$	☐	$
			$	☐	$
			$	☐	$
			$	☐	$

2d. Other Liabilities and Expenses   ☐ Does not apply

Include all other liabilities and expenses below. Choose from the types listed here:
- Alimony
- Child Support
- Separate Maintenance
- Job Related Expenses
- Other

	Monthly Payment
	$
	$
	$

Borrower Name:
Uniform Residential Loan Application
Freddie Mac Form 65 · Fannie Mae Form 1003
Effective 1/2021

Uniform Residential Loan Application [URLA], Page 4

Section 3: Financial Information — Real Estate. This section asks you to list all properties you currently own and what you owe on them. ☐ *I do not own any real estate*

3a. Property You Own If you are refinancing, list the property you are refinancing FIRST.

Address	Street								Unit #
	City				State	ZIP		Country	

Property Value	Status: Sold, Pending Sale, or Retained	Intended Occupancy: Investment, Primary Residence, Second Home, Other	Monthly Insurance, Taxes, Association Dues, etc. *if not included in Monthly Mortgage Payment*	For 2-4 Unit Primary or Investment Property	
				Monthly Rental Income	For LENDER to calculate: Net Monthly Rental Income
$			$	$	$

Mortgage Loans on this Property ☐ *Does not apply*

Creditor Name	Account Number	Monthly Mortgage Payment	Unpaid Balance	To be paid off at or before closing	Type: FHA, VA, Conventional, USDA-RD, Other	Credit Limit *(if applicable)*
		$	$	☐		$
		$	$	☐		$

3b. IF APPLICABLE, Complete Information for Additional Property ☐ *Does not apply*

Address	Street								Unit #
	City				State	ZIP		Country	

Property Value	Status: Sold, Pending Sale, or Retained	Intended Occupancy: Investment, Primary Residence, Other	Monthly Insurance, Taxes, Association Dues, etc. *if not included in Monthly Mortgage Payment*	For 2-4 Unit Primary or Investment Property	
				Monthly Rental Income	For LENDER to calculate: Net Monthly Rental Income
$			$	$	$

Mortgage Loans on this Property ☐ *Does not apply*

Creditor Name	Account Number	Monthly Mortgage Payment	Unpaid Balance	To be paid off at or before closing	Type: FHA, VA, Conventional, USDA-RD, Other	Credit Limit *(if applicable)*
		$	$	☐		$
		$	$	☐		$

3c. IF APPLICABLE, Complete Information for Additional Property ☐ *Does not apply*

Address	Street								Unit #
	City				State	ZIP		Country	

Property Value	Status: Sold, Pending Sale, or Retained	Intended Occupancy: Investment, Primary Residence, Second Home, Other	Monthly Insurance, Taxes, Association Dues, etc. *if not included in Monthly Mortgage Payment*	For 2-4 Unit Primary or Investment Property	
				Monthly Rental Income	For LENDER to calculate: Net Monthly Rental Income
$			$	$	$

Mortgage Loans on this Property ☐ *Does not apply*

Creditor Name	Account Number	Monthly Mortgage Payment	Unpaid Balance	To be paid off at or before closing	Type: FHA, VA, Conventional, USDA-RD, Other	Credit Limit *(if applicable)*
		$	$	☐		$
		$	$	☐		$

Borrower Name:
Uniform Residential Loan Application
Freddie Mac Form 65 • Fannie Mae Form 1003
Effective 1/2021

Uniform Residential Loan Application [URLA], Page 5

Section 4: Loan and Property Information. This section asks about the loan's purpose and the property you want to purchase or refinance.

4a. Loan and Property Information

Loan Amount $ _____

Loan Purpose ○ Purchase ○ Refinance ○ Other *(specify)* _____

Property Address Street _____ Unit # _____

City _____ State _____ ZIP _____ County _____

Number of Units _____ Property Value $ _____

Occupancy ○ Primary Residence ○ Second Home ○ Investment Property FHA Secondary Residence ☐

1. **Mixed-Use Property.** If you will occupy the property, will you set aside space within the property to operate your own business? *(e.g., daycare facility, medical office, beauty/barber shop)* ○ NO ○ YES

2. **Manufactured Home.** Is the property a manufactured home? *(e.g., a factory built dwelling built on a permanent chassis)* ○ NO ○ YES

4b. Other New Mortgage Loans on the Property You are Buying or Refinancing   ☐ Does not apply

Creditor Name	Lien Type	Monthly Payment	Loan Amount/ Amount to be Drawn	Credit Limit (if applicable)
	○ First Lien ○ Subordinate Lien	$	$	$
	○ First Lien ○ Subordinate Lien	$	$	$

4c. Rental Income on the Property You Want to Purchase   For Purchase Only   ☐ Does not apply

Complete if the property is a 2-4 Unit Primary Residence or an Investment Property	Amount
Expected Monthly Rental Income	$
For LENDER to calculate: Expected Net Monthly Rental Income	$

4d. Gifts or Grants You Have Been Given or Will Receive for this Loan   ☐ Does not apply

Include all gifts and grants below. Under Source, choose from the sources listed here:
- Community Nonprofit
- Employer
- Federal Agency
- Local Agency
- Relative
- Religious Nonprofit
- State Agency
- Unmarried Partner
- Lender
- Other

Asset Type: Cash Gift, Gift of Equity, Grant	Deposited/Not Deposited	Source – use list above	Cash or Market Value
	○ Deposited ○ Not Deposited		$
	○ Deposited ○ Not Deposited		$

Uniform Residential Loan Application [URLA], Page 6

Section 5: Declarations. This section asks you specific questions about the property, your funding, and your past financial history.

5a. About this Property and Your Money for this Loan

A. Will you occupy the property as your primary residence? If YES, have you had an ownership interest in another property in the last three years? If YES, complete (1) and (2) below: (1) What type of property did you own: primary residence (PR), FHA secondary residence (SR), second home (SH), or investment property (IP)? (2) How did you hold title to the property: by yourself (S), jointly with your spouse (SP), or jointly with another person (O)?	○ NO ○ YES ○ NO ○ YES _____ _____
B. If this is a Purchase Transaction: Do you have a family relationship or business affiliation with the seller of the property?	○ NO ○ YES
C. Are you borrowing any money for this real estate transaction (e.g., money for your closing costs or down payment) or obtaining any money from another party, such as the seller or realtor, that you have not disclosed on this loan application? If YES, what is the amount of this money?	○ NO ○ YES $_____
D. 1. Have you or will you be applying for a mortgage loan on another property (not the property securing this loan) on or before closing this transaction that is not disclosed on this loan application?	○ NO ○ YES
2. Have you or will you be applying for any new credit (e.g., installment loan, credit card, etc.) on or before closing this loan that is not disclosed on this application?	○ NO ○ YES
E. Will this property be subject to a lien that could take priority over the first mortgage lien, such as a clean energy lien paid through your property taxes (e.g., the Property Assessed Clean Energy Program)?	○ NO ○ YES

5b. About Your Finances

F. Are you a co-signer or guarantor on any debt or loan that is not disclosed on this application?	○ NO ○ YES
G. Are there any outstanding judgments against you?	○ NO ○ YES
H. Are you currently delinquent or in default on a Federal debt?	○ NO ○ YES
I. Are you a party to a lawsuit in which you potentially have any personal financial liability?	○ NO ○ YES
J. Have you conveyed title to any property in lieu of foreclosure in the past 7 years?	○ NO ○ YES
K. Within the past 7 years, have you completed a pre-foreclosure sale or short sale, whereby the property was sold to a third party and the Lender agreed to accept less than the outstanding mortgage balance due?	○ NO ○ YES
L. Have you had property foreclosed upon in the last 7 years?	○ NO ○ YES
M. Have you declared bankruptcy within the past 7 years? If YES, identify the type(s) of bankruptcy: ☐ Chapter 7 ☐ Chapter 11 ☐ Chapter 12 ☐ Chapter 13	○ NO ○ YES

Uniform Residential Loan Application [URLA], Page 7

Section 6: Acknowledgments and Agreements. This section tells you about your legal obligations when you sign this application.

Acknowledgments and Agreements

Definitions:
- "Lender" includes the Lender's agents, service providers, and any of their successors and assigns.
- "Other Loan Participants" includes (i) any actual or potential owners of a loan resulting from this application (the "Loan"), (ii) acquirers of any beneficial or other interest in the Loan, (iii) any mortgage insurer, (iv) any guarantor, (v) any servicer of the Loan, and (vi) any of these parties' service providers, successors or assigns.

I agree to, acknowledge, and represent the following:

(1) The Complete Information for this Application
- The information I have provided in this application is true, accurate, and complete as of the date I signed this application.
- If the information I submitted changes or I have new information before closing of the Loan, I must change and supplement this application, including providing any updated/supplemented real estate sales contract.
- For purchase transactions: The terms and conditions of any real estate sales contract signed by me in connection with this application are true, accurate, and complete to the best of my knowledge and belief. I have not entered into any other agreement, written or oral, in connection with this real estate transaction.
- The Lender and Other Loan Participants may rely on the information contained in the application before and after closing of the Loan.
- Any intentional or negligent misrepresentation of information may result in the imposition of:
  - (a) civil liability on me, including monetary damages, if a person suffers any loss because the person relied on any misrepresentation that I have made on this application, and/or
  - (b) criminal penalties on me including, but not limited to, fine or imprisonment or both under the provisions of Federal law (18 U.S.C. §§ 1001 et seq.).

(2) The Property's Security
The Loan I have applied for in this application will be secured by a mortgage or deed of trust which provides the Lender a security interest in the property described in this application.

(3) The Property's Appraisal, Value, and Condition
- Any appraisal or value of the property obtained by the Lender is for use by the Lender and Other Loan Participants.
- The Lender and Other Loan Participants have not made any representation or warranty, express or implied, to me about the property, its condition, or its value.

(4) Electronic Records and Signatures
- The Lender and Other Loan Participants may keep any paper record and/or electronic record of this application, whether or not the Loan is approved.

- If this application is created as (or converted into) an "electronic application", I consent to the use of "electronic records" and "electronic signatures" as the terms are defined in and governed by applicable Federal and/or state electronic transactions laws.
- I intend to sign and have signed this application either using my:
  - (a) electronic signature; or
  - (b) a written signature and agree that if a paper version of this application is converted into an electronic application, the application will be an electronic record, and the representation of my written signature on this application will be my binding electronic signature.
- I agree that the application, if delivered or transmitted to the Lender or Other Loan Participants as an electronic record with my electronic signature, will be as effective and enforceable as a paper application signed by me in writing.

(5) Delinquency
- The Lender and Other Loan Participants may report information about my account to credit bureaus. Late payments, missed payments, or other defaults on my account may be reflected in my credit report and will likely affect my credit score.
- If I have trouble making my payments I understand that I may contact a HUD-approved housing counseling organization for advice about actions I can take to meet my mortgage obligations.

(6) Authorization for Use and Sharing of Information
By signing below, in addition to the representations and agreements made above, I expressly authorize the Lender and Other Loan Participants to obtain, use, and share with each other (i) the loan application and related loan information and documentation, (ii) a consumer credit report on me, and (iii) my tax return information, as necessary to perform the actions listed below, for so long as they have an interest in my loan or its servicing:
- (a) process and underwrite my loan;
- (b) verify any data contained in my consumer credit report, my loan application and other information supporting my loan application;
- (c) inform credit and investment decisions by the Lender and Other Loan Participants;
- (d) perform audit, quality control, and legal compliance analysis and reviews;
- (e) perform analysis and modeling for risk assessments;
- (f) monitor the account for this loan for potential delinquencies and determine any assistance that may be available to me; and
- (g) other actions permissible under applicable law.

Borrower Signature _____   Date (mm/dd/yyyy) ____ / ____ / _____

Additional Borrower Signature _____   Date (mm/dd/yyyy) ____ / ____ / _____

Borrower Name: _____
Uniform Residential Loan Application
Freddie Mac Form 65 • Fannie Mae Form 1003
Effective 1/2021

Uniform Residential Loan Application [URLA], Page 8

Section 7: Military Service. This section asks questions about your (or your deceased spouse's) military service.

Military Service of Borrower

Military Service – Did you (or your deceased spouse) ever serve, or are you currently serving, in the United States Armed Forces? ○ NO ○ YES

If YES, check all that apply:
☐ Currently serving on active duty with projected expiration date of service/tour   / /   *(mm/dd/yyyy)*
☐ Currently retired, discharged, or separated from service
☐ Only period of service was as a non-activated member of the Reserve or National Guard
☐ Surviving spouse

Section 8: Demographic Information. This section asks about your ethnicity, sex, and race.

Demographic Information of Borrower

The purpose of collecting this information is to help ensure that all applicants are treated fairly and that the housing needs of communities and neighborhoods are being fulfilled. For residential mortgage lending, Federal law requires that we ask applicants for their demographic information (ethnicity, sex, and race) in order to monitor our compliance with equal credit opportunity, fair housing, and home mortgage disclosure laws. You are not required to provide this information, but are encouraged to do so. You may select one or more designations for "Ethnicity" and one or more designations for "Race." **The law provides that we may not discriminate** on the basis of this information, or on whether you choose to provide it. However, if you choose not to provide the information and you have made this application in person, Federal regulations require us to note your ethnicity, sex, and race on the basis of visual observation or surname. The law also provides that we may not discriminate on the basis of age or marital status information you provide in this application. If you do not wish to provide some or all of this information, please check below.

Ethnicity: *Check one or more*
☐ Hispanic or Latino
  ☐ Mexican   ☐ Puerto Rican   ☐ Cuban
  ☐ Other Hispanic or Latino – *Print origin:*

  For example: Argentinean, Colombian, Dominican, Nicaraguan, Salvadoran, Spaniard, and so on.
☐ Not Hispanic or Latino
☐ I do not wish to provide this information

Sex
☐ Female
☐ Male
☐ I do not wish to provide this information

Race: *Check one or more*
☐ American Indian or Alaska Native – *Print name of enrolled or principal tribe :*
☐ Asian
  ☐ Asian Indian   ☐ Chinese   ☐ Filipino
  ☐ Japanese   ☐ Korean   ☐ Vietnamese
  ☐ Other Asian – *Print race:*
  For example: Hmong, Laotian, Thai, Pakistani, Cambodian, and so on.
☐ Black or African American
☐ Native Hawaiian or Other Pacific Islander
  ☐ Native Hawaiian   ☐ Guamanian or Chamorro   ☐ Samoan
  ☐ Other Pacific Islander – *Print race:*
  For example: Fijian, Tongan, and so on.
☐ White
☐ I do not wish to provide this information

To Be Completed by Financial Institution (for application taken in person):

Was the ethnicity of the Borrower collected on the basis of visual observation or surname? ○ NO ○ YES
Was the sex of the Borrower collected on the basis of visual observation or surname? ○ NO ○ YES
Was the race of the Borrower collected on the basis of visual observation or surname? ○ NO ○ YES

The Demographic Information was provided through:

○ Face-to-Face Interview *(includes Electronic Media w/ Video Component)*   ○ Telephone Interview   ○ Fax or Mail   ○ Email or Internet

Borrower Name: _____
Uniform Residential Loan Application
Freddie Mac Form 65 · Fannie Mae Form 1003
Effective 1/2021

202

Uniform Residential Loan Application [URLA], Page 9

Section 9: Loan Originator Information. To be completed by your **Loan Originator**.

Loan Originator Information

Loan Originator Organization Name _____

Address _____

Loan Originator Organization NMLSR ID# _____ State License ID# _____

Loan Originator Name _____

Loan Originator NMLSR ID# _____ State License ID# _____

Email _____ Phone (_____) _____ – _____

Signature _____ Date (mm/dd/yyyy) _____ / _____ / _____

APPENDIX C

Loan Estimate [LE], Page 1

Save this Loan Estimate to compare with your Closing Disclosure.

Loan Estimate

DATE ISSUED
APPLICANTS

PROPERTY
EST. PROP. VALUE

LOAN TERM
PURPOSE
PRODUCT
LOAN TYPE ☐ Conventional ☐ FHA ☐ VA ☐ _____
LOAN ID #
RATE LOCK ☐ NO ☐ YES, until

Before closing, your interest rate, points, and lender credits can change unless you lock the interest rate. All other estimated closing costs expire on

Loan Terms	Can this amount increase after closing?
Loan Amount	
Interest Rate	
Monthly Principal & Interest See Projected Payments below for your Estimated Total Monthly Payment	
	Does the loan have these features?
Prepayment Penalty	
Balloon Payment	

Projected Payments	
Payment Calculation	
Principal & Interest	
Mortgage Insurance	
Estimated Escrow Amount can increase over time	
Estimated Total Monthly Payment	

Estimated Taxes, Insurance & Assessments Amount can increase over time	This estimate includes In escrow? ☐ Property Taxes ☐ Homeowner's Insurance ☐ Other: See Section G on page 2 for escrowed property costs. You must pay for other property costs separately.

Costs at Closing	
Estimated Closing Costs	Includes in Loan Costs + in Other Costs – in Lender Credits. See page 2 for details.
Estimated Cash to Close	Includes Closing Costs. See Calculating Cash to Close on page 2 for details.

Visit www.consumerfinance.gov/mortgage-estimate for general information and tools.

LOAN ESTIMATE   PAGE 1 OF 3 · LOAN ID #

Loan Estimate [LE], Page 2

Closing Cost Details

Loan Costs

A. Origination Charges
% of Loan Amount (Points)

B. Services You Cannot Shop For

C. Services You Can Shop For

D. TOTAL LOAN COSTS (A + B + C)

Other Costs

E. Taxes and Other Government Fees
Recording Fees and Other Taxes
Transfer Taxes

F. Prepaids
Homeowner's Insurance Premium (months)
Mortgage Insurance Premium (months)
Prepaid Interest (per day for days @)
Property Taxes (months)

G. Initial Escrow Payment at Closing
Homeowner's Insurance   per month for   mo.
Mortgage Insurance   per month for   mo.
Property Taxes   per month for   mo.

H. Other

I. TOTAL OTHER COSTS (E + F + G + H)

J. TOTAL CLOSING COSTS
D + I
Lender Credits

Calculating Cash to Close

Total Closing Costs (J)
Closing Costs Financed (Paid from your Loan Amount)
Down Payment/Funds from Borrower
Deposit
Funds for Borrower
Seller Credits
Adjustments and Other Credits
Estimated Cash to Close

Adjustable Payment (AP) Table

Interest Only Payments?	
Optional Payments?	
Step Payments?	
Seasonal Payments?	
Monthly Principal and Interest Payments	
First Change/Amount	
Subsequent Changes	
Maximum Payment	

Adjustable Interest Rate (AIR) Table

Index + Margin	
Initial Interest Rate	
Minimum/Maximum Interest Rate	
Change Frequency	
First Change	
Subsequent Changes	
Limits on Interest Rate Changes	
First Change	
Subsequent Changes	

Loan Estimate [LE], Page 3

Additional Information About This Loan

LENDER
NMLS/___ LICENSE ID
LOAN OFFICER
NMLS/___ LICENSE ID
EMAIL
PHONE

MORTGAGE BROKER
NMLS/___ LICENSE ID
LOAN OFFICER
NMLS/___ LICENSE ID
EMAIL
PHONE

Comparisons	Use these measures to compare this loan with other loans.
In 5 Years	Total you will have paid in principal, interest, mortgage insurance, and loan costs. Principal you will have paid off.
Annual Percentage Rate (APR)	Your costs over the loan term expressed as a rate. This is not your interest rate.
Total Interest Percentage (TIP)	The total amount of interest that you will pay over the loan term as a percentage of your loan amount.

Other Considerations

Appraisal
We may order an appraisal to determine the property's value and charge you for this appraisal. We will promptly give you a copy of any appraisal, even if your loan does not close. You can pay for an additional appraisal for your own use at your own cost.

Assumption
If you sell or transfer this property to another person, we
☐ will allow, under certain conditions, this person to assume this loan on the original terms.
☐ will not allow assumption of this loan on the original terms.

Homeowner's Insurance
This loan requires homeowner's insurance on the property, which you may obtain from a company of your choice that we find acceptable.

Late Payment
If your payment is more than ___ days late, we will charge a late fee of _____

Loan Acceptance
You do not have to accept this loan because you have received this form or signed a loan application.

Refinance
Refinancing this loan will depend on your future financial situation, the property value, and market conditions. You may not be able to refinance this loan.

Servicing
We intend
☐ to service your loan. If so, you will make your payments to us.
☐ to transfer servicing of your loan.

LOAN ESTIMATE

PAGE 3 OF 3 • LOAN ID #

APPENDIX D

Closing Disclosure [CD], Page 1

Closing Disclosure

This form is a statement of final loan terms and closing costs. Compare this document with your Loan Estimate.

Closing Information	Transaction Information	Loan Information
Date Issued	Borrower	Loan Term
Closing Date		Purpose
Disbursement Date		Product
Settlement Agent	Seller	
File #		Loan Type ☐ Conventional ☐ FHA ☐ VA ☐ _____
Property	Lender	Loan ID #
Estimated Prop. Value		MIC #

Loan Terms

	Can this amount increase after closing?
Loan Amount	
Interest Rate	
Monthly Principal & Interest *See Projected Payments below for your Estimated Total Monthly Payment*	

	Does the loan have these features?
Prepayment Penalty	
Balloon Payment	

Projected Payments

Payment Calculation	
Principal & Interest	
Mortgage Insurance	
Estimated Escrow *Amount can increase over time*	
Estimated Total Monthly Payment	

Estimated Taxes, Insurance & Assessments *Amount can increase over time* *See page 4 for details*	**This estimate includes** ☐ Property Taxes ☐ Homeowner's Insurance ☐ Other: **In escrow?** *See Escrow Account on page 4 for details. You must pay for other property costs separately.*

Costs at Closing

Closing Costs	Includes _____ in Loan Costs + _____ in Other Costs – _____ in Lender Credits. See page 2 for details.
Cash to Close	Includes Closing Costs. See Calculating Cash to Close on page 3 for details.

CLOSING DISCLOSURE

Closing Disclosure [CD], Page 2

Closing Cost Details

Loan Costs	Borrower-Paid		Seller-Paid		Paid by Others
	At Closing	Before Closing	At Closing	Before Closing	
A. Origination Charges					
01 % of Loan Amount (Points)					
02					
03					
04					
05					
06					
07					
08					
B. Services Borrower Did Not Shop For					
01					
02					
03					
04					
05					
06					
07					
08					
09					
10					
C. Services Borrower Did Shop For					
01					
02					
03					
04					
05					
06					
07					
08					
D. TOTAL LOAN COSTS (Borrower-Paid)					
Loan Costs Subtotals (A + B + C)					

Other Costs					
E. Taxes and Other Government Fees					
01 Recording Fees Deed: Mortgage:					
02					
F. Prepaids					
01 Homeowner's Insurance Premium (mo.)					
02 Mortgage Insurance Premium (mo.)					
03 Prepaid Interest (per day from to)					
04 Property Taxes (mo.)					
05					
G. Initial Escrow Payment at Closing					
01 Homeowner's Insurance per month for mo.					
02 Mortgage Insurance per month for mo.					
03 Property Taxes per month for mo.					
04					
05					
06					
07					
08 Aggregate Adjustment					
H. Other					
01					
02					
03					
04					
05					
06					
07					
08					
I. TOTAL OTHER COSTS (Borrower-Paid)					
Other Costs Subtotals (E + F + G + H)					
J. TOTAL CLOSING COSTS (Borrower-Paid)					
Closing Costs Subtotals (D + I)					
Lender Credits					

CLOSING DISCLOSURE

PAGE 2 OF 5 · LOAN ID #

Closing Disclosure [CD], Page 3

Calculating Cash to Close	Loan Estimate	Final	Use this table to see what has changed from your Loan Estimate. Did this change?
Total Closing Costs (J)			
Closing Costs Paid Before Closing			
Closing Costs Financed (Paid from your Loan Amount)			
Down Payment/Funds from Borrower			
Deposit			
Funds for Borrower			
Seller Credits			
Adjustments and Other Credits			
Cash to Close			

Summaries of Transactions — Use this table to see a summary of your transaction.

BORROWER'S TRANSACTION

K. Due from Borrower at Closing
01 Sale Price of Property
02 Sale Price of Any Personal Property Included in Sale
03 Closing Costs Paid at Closing (J)
04

Adjustments
05
06
07

Adjustments for Items Paid by Seller in Advance
08 City/Town Taxes   to
09 County Taxes   to
10 Assessments   to
11
12
13
14
15

L. Paid Already by or on Behalf of Borrower at Closing
01 Deposit
02 Loan Amount
03 Existing Loan(s) Assumed or Taken Subject to
04
05 Seller Credit
Other Credits
06
07

Adjustments
08
09
10
11

Adjustments for Items Unpaid by Seller
12 City/Town Taxes   to
13 County Taxes   to
14 Assessments   to
15
16
17

CALCULATION
Total Due from Borrower at Closing (K)
Total Paid Already by or on Behalf of Borrower at Closing (L)
Cash to Close ☐ From ☐ To Borrower

SELLER'S TRANSACTION

M. Due to Seller at Closing
01 Sale Price of Property
02 Sale Price of Any Personal Property Included in Sale
03
04
05
06
07
08

Adjustments for Items Paid by Seller in Advance
09 City/Town Taxes   to
10 County Taxes   to
11 Assessments   to
12
13
14
15
16

N. Due from Seller at Closing
01 Excess Deposit
02 Closing Costs Paid at Closing (J)
03 Existing Loan(s) Assumed or Taken Subject to
04 Payoff of First Mortgage Loan
05 Payoff of Second Mortgage Loan
06
07
08 Seller Credit
09
10
11
12

Adjustments for Items Unpaid by Seller
14 City/Town Taxes   to
15 County Taxes   to
16 Assessments   to
17
18
19

CALCULATION
Total Due to Seller at Closing (M)
Total Due from Seller at Closing (N)
Cash ☐ From ☐ To Seller

Closing Disclosure [CD], Page 4

Additional Information About This Loan

Loan Disclosures

Assumption

If you sell or transfer this property to another person, your lender

☐ will allow, under certain conditions, this person to assume this loan on the original terms.

☐ will not allow assumption of this loan on the original terms.

Demand Feature

Your loan

☐ has a demand feature, which permits your lender to require early repayment of the loan. You should review your note for details.

☐ does not have a demand feature.

Late Payment

If your payment is more than ___ days late, your lender will charge a late fee of ___

Negative Amortization (Increase in Loan Amount)

Under your loan terms, you

☐ are scheduled to make monthly payments that do not pay all of the interest due that month. As a result, your loan amount will increase (negatively amortize), and your loan amount will likely become larger than your original loan amount. Increases in your loan amount lower the equity you have in this property.

☐ may have monthly payments that do not pay all of the interest due that month. If you do, your loan amount will increase (negatively amortize), and, as a result, your loan amount may become larger than your original loan amount. Increases in your loan amount lower the equity you have in this property.

☐ do not have a negative amortization feature.

Partial Payments

Your lender

☐ may accept payments that are less than the full amount due (partial payments) and apply them to your loan.

☐ may hold them in a separate account until you pay the rest of the payment, and then apply the full payment to your loan.

☐ does not accept any partial payments.

If this loan is sold, your new lender may have a different policy.

Security Interest

You are granting a security interest in _____

_____

You may lose this property if you do not make your payments or satisfy other obligations for this loan.

Escrow Account

For now, your loan

☐ will have an escrow account (also called an "impound" or "trust" account) to pay the property costs listed below. Without an escrow account, you would pay directly, possibly in one or two large payments a year. Your lender may be liable for penalties and interest for failing to make a payment.

Escrow		
Escrowed Property Costs over Year 1		Estimated total amount over year 1 for your escrowed property costs:
Non-Escrowed Property Costs over Year 1		Estimated total amount over year 1 for your non-escrowed property costs
		You may have other property costs.
Initial Escrow Payment		A cushion for the escrow account you pay at closing. See Section G on page 2.
Monthly Escrow Payment		The amount included in your total monthly payment.

☐ will not have an escrow account because ☐ you declined it ☐ your lender does not offer one. You must directly pay your property costs, such as taxes and homeowner's insurance. Contact your lender to ask if your loan can have an escrow account.

No Escrow		
Estimated Property Costs over Year 1		Estimated total amount over year 1. You must pay these costs directly, possibly in one or two large payments a year.
Escrow Waiver Fee		

In the future,

Your property costs may change and, as a result, your escrow payment may change. You may be able to cancel your escrow account, but if you do, you must pay your property costs directly. If you fail to pay your property taxes, your state or local government may (1) impose fines and penalties or (2) place a tax lien on this property. If you fail to pay any of your property costs, your lender may (1) add the amounts to your loan balance, (2) add an escrow account to your loan, or (3) require you to pay for property insurance that the lender buys on your behalf, which likely would cost more and provide fewer benefits than what you could buy on your own.

Adjustable Payment (AP) Table

Interest Only Payments?	
Optional Payments?	
Step Payments?	
Seasonal Payments?	
Monthly Principal and Interest Payments	
First Change/Amount	
Subsequent Changes	
Maximum Payment	

Adjustable Interest Rate (AIR) Table

Index + Margin	
Initial Interest Rate	
Minimum/Maximum Interest Rate	
Change Frequency	
First Change	
Subsequent Changes	
Limits on Interest Rate Changes	
First Change	
Subsequent Changes	

Closing Disclosure [CD], Page 5

Loan Calculations

Total of Payments. Total you will have paid after you make all payments of principal, interest, mortgage insurance, and loan costs, as scheduled.

Finance Charge. The dollar amount the loan will cost you.

Amount Financed. The loan amount available after paying your upfront finance charge.

Annual Percentage Rate (APR). Your costs over the loan term expressed as a rate. This is not your interest rate.

Total Interest Percentage (TIP). The total amount of interest that you will pay over the loan term as a percentage of your loan amount.

Questions? If you have questions about the loan terms or costs on this form, use the contact information below. To get more information or make a complaint, contact the Consumer Financial Protection Bureau at www.consumerfinance.gov/mortgage-closing

Other Disclosures

Appraisal
If the property was appraised for your loan, your lender is required to give you a copy at no additional cost at least 3 days before closing. If you have not yet received it, please contact your lender at the information listed below.

Contract Details
See your note and security instrument for information about
- what happens if you fail to make your payments,
- what is a default on the loan,
- situations in which your lender can require early repayment of the loan, and
- the rules for making payments before they are due.

Liability after Foreclosure
If your lender forecloses on this property and the foreclosure does not cover the amount of unpaid balance on this loan,
☐ state law may protect you from liability for the unpaid balance. If you refinance or take on any additional debt on this property, you may lose this protection and have to pay any debt remaining even after foreclosure. You may want to consult a lawyer for more information.
☐ state law does not protect you from liability for the unpaid balance.

Loan Acceptance
You do not have to accept this loan because you have received this form or signed a loan application.

Refinance
Refinancing this loan will depend on your future financial situation, the property value, and market conditions. You may not be able to refinance this loan.

Tax Deductions
If you borrow more than this property is worth, the interest on the loan amount above this property's fair market value is not deductible from your federal income taxes. You should consult a tax advisor for more information.

Contact Information

	Lender	Mortgage Broker	Real Estate Broker (B)	Real Estate Broker (S)	Settlement Agent
Name					
Address					
NMLS ID					
__ License ID					
Contact					
Contact NMLS ID					
Contact __ License ID					
Email					
Phone					

INDEX

BIBLIOGRAPHY

2023 Employer Health Benefits Survey. (2023, October 18). Retrieved January 7, 2025, from KFF: https://www.kff.org/report-section/ehbs-2023-section-1-cost-of-health-insurance/

30 Year Fixed Rate Mortgages. (2025, January 15). Retrieved January 15, 2025, from Mortgage News Daily: https://www.mortgagenewsdaily.com/mortgage-rates/30-year-fixed

Average Home Owners Insurance Cost. (2024, November 13). Retrieved November 25, 2024, from Bankrate: https://www.bankrate.com/insurance/homeowners-insurance/homeowners-insurance-cost/

Ball, L. J. (2024, November 18). Chief Executive Officer, Texas Homeowners Association Management. (J. Hohman, Interviewer)

Board of Governors of the Federal Reserve System (US). (2025, January 18). *Market Yield on U.S. Treasury Securities at 10-Year Constant Maturity, Quoted on an Investment Basis [DGS10], retrieved from FRED.* Retrieved from Federal Reserve Bank of St. Louis: https://fred.stlouisfed.org/series/DGS10

Characteristics of New Housing, Data. (2024, June 3). Retrieved December 2, 2024, from U.S. Census Bureau: https://www.census.gov/construction/chars/current.html

Consumer Expenditures and Income: Overview. (2022, September 12). Retrieved January 14, 2025, from U.S Bureau of Labor Statistics: https://www.bls.gov/opub/hom/cex/home.htm

Consumer Financial Protection Bureau. (2023, August 28). *What happens when a mortgage lender checks my credit?* Retrieved October 8, 2024, from ConsumerFinance.gov: https://www.consumerfinance.gov/ask-cfpb/what-exactly-happens-when-a-mortgage-lender-checks-my-credit-en-2005/

Fabozzi, F. J. (1993, 1997). *Fixed Income Mathematics.* New York: McGraw-Hill.

Fabozzi, F. J. (2001, 1995). *The Handbook of Mortgage-Backed Securities.* New York: McGraw-Hill.

Fram, W. S., Gerardi, K., Sexton, D., & Tracy, J. (2020). *Ability to repay a mortgage: Assessing the relationship between default, debt-to-income.* Dallas: Federal Reserve Bank of Dallas; Federal Reserve Bank of Atlanta. Retrieved from https://www.dallasfed.org/research/economics/2020/032 4

Freddie Mac. (2025, January 18). *30-Year Fixed Rate Mortgage Average in the United States [MORTGAGE30US], retrieved from FRED.* Retrieved from Federal Reserve Bank of St. Louis: https://fred.stlouisfed.org/series/MORTGAGE30US#

hud.gov. (2023, February 22). Retrieved from U.S. Department of Housing and Urban Development: https://www.hud.gov/sites/dfiles/OCHCO/documents/202 3-05hsgml.pdf

Kagan, J. (2024, June 21). *LIBOR: What Was the London Interbank Offered Rate, and How Was It Used?* Retrieved from Investopedia: https://www.investopedia.com/terms/l/libor.asp

Keynes, J. M. (1953). *The General Theory of Employment, Interest, and Money.* Orlando: Harcourt.

Milliman, Inc. (2024). *Analysis of Claims and Claims-Related Losses in the Land Title Insurance Industry.* New York, NY: Milliman, Inc. Retrieved from https://www.alta.org/media/pdf/240517-analysis-of-claims-and-claims-related-losses-in-the-land-title-insurance-industry.pdf

National Association of REALTORS Research Group. (2024). *2024 Member Profile.* Washington, DC: National Association of REALTORS Research Group. Retrieved from https://www.nar.realtor/sites/default/files/documents/2024-nar-member-profile-highlights-07-10-2024.pdf

Property Owners' Associations. (2024, December 2). Retrieved December 2, 2024, from Texas State Law Library: https://guides.sll.texas.gov/property-owners-associations/assessments-foreclosure

Roberson, J., & McMeans, K. (2024, February 7). *Texas Housing Insight.* Retrieved January 15, 2025, from Texas A&M University Texas Real Estate Research Center: https://trerc.tamu.edu/wp-content/uploads/files/PDFs/Articles/2120-202402.pdf

Ryan, C. (2024, October 30). Wall Street Home Buying is Mixed Blessing. *The Wall Street Journal.*

S&P Dow Jones Indices LLC. (2024, November 12). *S&P CoreLogic Case-Shiller U.S. National Home Price Index [CSUSHPINSA].* Retrieved November 12, 2024, from FRED, Federal Reserve Bank of St. Louis: https://fred.stlouisfed.org/series/CSUSHPINSA

Saltford Manor House. (2025, January 18). Retrieved from Saltford Environment Group: https://www.saltfordenvironmentgroup.org.uk/history/history004.html

Selling Guide. (2024, December 11). Retrieved December 11, 2024, from Fannie Mae: https://selling-guide.fanniemae.com/

Sklansky, D. (1987). *The Theory of Poker.* Henderson: Two Plus Two Publishing LLC.

Stanley, T. J. (2010). *The Millionaire Next Door: The Surprising Secrets of America's Wealthy.* Lanham: Taylor Trade Publishing. Retrieved from https://themillionairenextdoor.com/

Thoreau, H. D. (1854). *Walden.* Boston: Ticknor and Fields.

U.S. Bureau of Labor Statistics. (2024, November 12). *Consumer Price Index for All Urban Consumers: Shelter in U.S. City Average [CUSR0000SAH1].* Retrieved November 12, 2024, from FRED, Federal Reserve Bank of St. Louis: https://fred.stlouisfed.org/series/CUSR0000SAH1

U.S. Census Bureau. (2024, November 12). *Homeownership Rate in the United States [RHORUSQ156N].* Retrieved November 12, 2024, from FRED, Federal Reserve Bank of St. Louis: https://fred.stlouisfed.org/series/RHORUSQ156N

U.S. Department of Housing and Urban Development Office of Policy Development and Research. (2017, August 14). *https://www.huduser.gov/portal/pdredge/pdr-edge-featd-article-081417.html.* Retrieved October 2024

Yushkov, A. (2024, August 20). *Property Taxes by State and County, 2024.* Retrieved November 15, 2024, from Tax Foundation: https://taxfoundation.org/data/all/state/property-taxes-by-state-county-2024/

ABOUT THE AUTHOR

Jaye Hohman founded Hohman Finance LLC in 2024 following ten years of originating and managing mortgage origination teams in Dallas. Prior to that, he led mortgage bond investment banking and trading activity in New York City. His analytic strategies have yielded excellent results for both institutional and consumer clients for over 25 years.

Born and raised in Indiana, Jaye Hohman began his Wall Street career in 1996 brokering US Treasurys in the bond pits at The World Trade Center. Over the next fifteen years he developed his craft of Mortgage-Backed Securities [MBS] while at Bear Stearns and other primary and secondary dealers.

Throughout that time, he built a career advising institutional money managers how to improve their asset/liability management strategies utilizing Collateralized Mortgage Obligations (CMOs) in their investment portfolios. He eventually headed several MBS derivative trading desks and led the investment banking platform of a foreign mortgage securitization conduit.

Since 2014, Jaye has originated home loans and supervised teams of residential mortgage loan originators on consumer direct, retail and wholesale lending platforms in Dallas.

His range of experience in the mortgage industry provides a unique perspective and cohesive understanding of how to maximize the financial benefits of mortgages while limiting the interest rate risk for both consumers and investors.

www.ingramcontent.com/pod-product-compliance
Lightning Source LLC
Chambersburg PA
CBHW071200210326
41597CB00016B/1611